MW01202154

rockbench
PUBLISHING

courageous thought leadership content

Managing (Right

for the First Time

A Field Guide for Doing it Well

David C. Baker

RockBench Publishing Corp—Nashville

RockBench Publishing Corp.
6101 Stillmeadow Dr., Nashville, TN 37211
www.rockbench.com

Printed in the United States of America
First edition, 2010

Published simultaneously in electronic format

Library of Congress Control Number: 2010905800

ISBN-13: 978-1-60544-002-6

1   2   3   4   5   6   7   8   9

For Julie, Jonathan, & Nathan

You've shaped my thinking through countless
times of connecting at an authentic level

Thank you

Table of Contents

Preface

We've all heard those jokes about how it's harder to get a driver's license than to become a parent, right? Well, it takes even less to become a manager. One day you aren't and one day you are. You might not have seen it coming, and you probably didn't get any training even if there was a slow build up to that eventful (or fateful) day.

What happens when we don't get the managing thing right? Well, I guess sometimes people die when the anger builds to the point where the co-worker brings that gun back to work and then shows up on CNN. (The amount of workplace violence alone should give us pause.) But normally, the results are simply grouchy managers, disgruntled employees, and unremarkable business results.

That may not seem all that significant in relation to the co-worker gone berserk, except that bad management is a lot more widespread than violent employees.

Think about it. You spend an enormous percentage of your life at work. Your circle of friends comes largely from workplace connections. And finally, what do you whine about the most after you get home after a long day? A boss who isn't managing or a co-worker who isn't being managed. So this is worth talking about.

We're humans, after all, and at its core, managing is essentially a human activity. As impactful as it is, it's still sloppy, never ending, unclear, and satisfying only at unpredictable moments.

That's why you don't find many books on the topic, by the way. Because it is essentially human, there's little science to it. What's more, everyone has a different style of managing and the notion of corralling all those "best practices" into some useful tome makes as much sense as asking all the best song writers in the world to divulge their best practices.

No, managing is individual, and that's because it flows from who we are as individual people. What that means is that the best we can do is get the core principles right and then forget about the rest. That's what this book is about: the core principles for first time managers. If you get those right, you'll figure the rest of it out in time.

The truth is that figuring it out is part of the reward for managing. There are many times when the light will go on in your own eyes and the resulting epiphany will deepen your motivation to do it right.

But remember that "managing is individual" on the receiving end, too. By that I mean that beyond the core concepts (which should never change), you'll want to tailor your management to the individuals being managed.

So we're going to talk about two big concepts, really. The first will revolve around the core principles you'll need to follow to get it right the first time. What you build on those core principles will depend on who you are as a person. But you must get the basic principles down, just like any athlete. Experimentation before mastering the core principles is irresponsible. Experimentation after mastering the core principles is a satisfying thing to watch.

Most of this book is about those core principles, but we'll touch on the second core concept toward the end: managing others individually without violating those core principles. You'll only be free to do that once you've mastered the basics. Again, like any professional athlete, the basics must be automatic to free up your brain for the extraordinary things. What does any good coach do if a team is struggling? Drag them back to the basics, which are the foundation for personalization.

So if you are a first-time manager who wants to get it right out of the gate, or a long-time manager who wants to get it right for the first time, this book is for you. I wouldn't presume to tell you what to do with this book now that you bought it or received it as a gift, but may I make some suggestions on how to benefit from it? Here we go.

First, read it when you need it. Unless you're itching somewhere, a scratch is just irritating and unconnected to a real need. So you might want to read this at the outset of this managing journey when you are truly mystified about how you're going to manage this person that you had lunch with just yesterday as a peer, where you whined about the boss together. Or you might want to read this right after you've been criticized, fairly or not, by your boss or one of your charges. All this to say that there must be some motivation for you to listen and then change your behavior.

Second, read it when you can get through it in one or two sittings, like on vacation, on an airplane, or just before a planning/management retreat when you have to be a tad introspective and lead a discussion.

13

Third, read it when you are so engaged that you don't need to take notes. If you are engaged, you will remember the important things you read as you look at a thought from multiple angles, wrap it in your own experience, and store it as your own "aha" moment.

Fourth, read it in a reckless mood, like the mood you have to be in to really effectively clean out a garage. Don't think too deeply about anything—follow your first instincts and pitch the thought or keep it, but don't noodle anything to death. There is no magic, here, just a basic guide designed to point you in the right direction while you blaze your own path through this management jungle.

There you go. Now let me explain where this comes from so you'll have some context.

I wish I could tell you that I'm one of the world's best managers and I'm just doing a mind dump so you can be as good as me. If I did that, I'd have to make sure no one who knows me got a copy of this book because I'd be run off the planet.

But you do deserve to know where this comes from just like you deserve to see the Doctor's diploma on the wall.

First, the material from this book comes from my experience as an employee. From what I can remember, I've worked at about fifteen places. Most were the odd summer jobs, but the remaining handful of jobs were "real" jobs where I stayed for years. I've had great bosses, evil bosses, and mainly normal bosses, but I've learned things from all of them.

Second, the material comes from my experience as a manager, either as a pure manager or a manager/owner. I've held management positions at three companies that I didn't own, and I've been an owner/manager at two companies.

Third, the material comes from my experience as a parent. Julie and I have two grown boys and probably nothing taught me more about management than being responsible for guiding them. I learned from the things I did well and the things I failed at.

Fourth, the material comes from the more than five hundred small businesses I've worked with over the last sixteen years, spending extensive time with each founder. In addition, each employee of those companies has completed an exhaustive on-line survey followed by a face-to face interview with most of them. I've heard the manager's side, heard the employee's side, and then seen the truth with my own eyes. I've helped countless employees transition to managers, often because I saw something, blessed the decision, and then watched in the background as the person flourished. Or even owners, who suddenly found themselves facing a much greater management role. I've helped fire managers that weren't cutting it and I've stepped between an owner and a manager to prevent an unfair dismissal. I've had more than eight thousand conversations with people about how they want to be managed, what they wish were different, and how much they appreciate some particular aspect of a manager's style.

Fifth, the material comes from speaking on management topics to audiences large and small, where it has always been my practice to take any question from the audience. Standing naked, so to speak, in front of thousands of people and having to explain/defend a management concept leaves you no option but to know what you believe and be able to articulate it.

So that's it. Notable by their absence from this list, as you've probably already noticed, are two things: formal education and books on the subject of management. I have more than enough of the former (six years of my life in graduate school that I'd love to have back, just for starters), but I've never wanted to learn all that much from professors in a sterile environment. It's great for academia, but it's not all that great for life. What I do value from education is the discipline required to actually graduate, as well as the opportunity to make so many friends in the process.

And books, well, what can I say. Besides what you're cradling gratefully in your hands at the moment, most are full of fluff, fad, or fantasy. There are a few notable exceptions, though, like this one. But mainly they don't resonate with my own experience and so I don't know what to do with the suggestions.

Finally, let me thank you for interacting with these ideas. As you read this and as you apply it to your situation, please continue the discussion with your fellow managers, and do let me know what you discover along the path.

Now to the core concepts of managing well.

Introduction

You haven't noticed yet, but there are several little red light points on your chest. And no, it's not because the neighbor kid is playing with the slide presentation pointer that fell out of your briefcase last night when you stumbled home, finally, after a hard day at work. It's more that you're in the cross hairs of one or more people who are watching very carefully how you react in the next few weeks.

You've crossed a threshold, see, by either managing people for the first time, or trying to do it right for the first time. This is your chance. You've experienced a seminal event in your life by entering the "management" room that you've only heard of in the past. You've criticized the people who have occupied this room without ever knowing what it was really like to be in their shoes.

Now you get to find out, and you get to do it better. Are you ready? Have you been paying attention? Do you understand the minuses that will come with the pluses? It's a wonderful journey, but it's not without difficulty.

I can't remember much about the first time I managed people. Maybe for you it was like my experience, a more gradual transition in that I was managing them in reality long before I was managing them officially, and being promoted was more about recognizing what was already taking place. That's probably the best way for it to happen.

But I probably don't remember that first time simply because our culture doesn't value management all that highly. You don't read about great managers like you read about great athletes, and so we aren't accustomed to thinking of the entry to management as some sort of anniversary.

It is, though, because it changes your life. It may not change your life to the same extent that childbirth, marriage, divorce, or death will change your life, but it certainly sets a course with all sorts of implications for your life.

This is a change, and how you react to it will affect your happiness, relationships, health, and wealth. It will also have a strong impact on the people you manage.

You do realize that, right? Twenty years from now, let me sit down with one of your current clients and ask them about you, your impact, and what they learned. Chances are they won't even be able to dredge a name out of their murky memories. The same is true of your vendors.

But let me do that with one of your current employees in twenty years and they'll remember you for sure. Hopefully it'll be for the right reasons, and that's the opportunity that is in front of you.

1

Who Managers Are and How You Become One

What is management, anyway? In the context of this book, I'm going to define it as taking responsibility for the performance and output of another employee in a business setting. There is obviously some overlap between that and leadership, and in many cases we can use the terms interchangeably, but in the end it boils down to being responsible for those two things—performance and output—and it relates to doing so with people in a business setting.

With that in mind, I want to make some statements about management to set the stage for our later discussion. Unless we're on the same page here at the outset, we're likely to be miles apart at the end of this journey.

YOUR APTITUDE COMES LARGELY
FROM THE CHOICES YOU'VE ALREADY MADE

I'll start by noting that management is not natural, and there are no "natural born" managers. Good management comes primarily from who you are as a person, and if you've made the right choices as you've responded to the circumstances you've encountered, there is a higher likelihood that you'll be a good manager. That's the first point, and it's a very important one.

Who you are as a person stems from the choices you have made in the circumstances you have faced. You have had precious little choice about some of those circumstances, but you have had all sorts of freedom in deciding how you would respond to those circumstances. All those little choices added together make up who you are.

So you live with that reality. It is what it is, and there's no changing the past. If the few big decisions and the many little decisions you have made were good ones, you're probably closer to being a good manager out of the gate and maybe all it will take is some good advice from this book and a few trusted friends, along with a huge dose of more self-awareness.

At the other end of the spectrum, you might be a downright evil person soon to be an evil manager. I'm not worried about that, though, because there's no way you'd be reading this book. What's more likely is that you are ready, and just need a little help, or you aren't ready but are quite willing to start making better choices.

I have to say that from a cold, statistical viewpoint, the odds of you changing significantly as a person just because you are a manager are not all that good. The additional power and isolation that will come your way will be severe tests of your character. But if you've been selected for management by a good manager, you can take solace in the fact that he or she sees something in you that you may not even see in yourself. This is good news, and it means that maybe you can grow into this position that is being carved out for you.

On the other hand, if you received a battlefield promotion (defined as nobody's first choice until the person who was the first choice got killed unexpectedly and now you are the first choice), then all bets are off. Or if you were chosen for a management position by someone who is a bad manager, it's just as grim. Not just because their judgment is suspect, but also because they won't necessarily support your new management role properly.

All this to say that you have to be ready, nearly ready, or willing to make a lot of changes to be ready if you want to be a good manager, and that what you've done since you started making choices has a lot more to do with your aptitude for management than anything your DNA might say.

IF YOU HAVE MADE GOOD CHOICES, MANAGEMENT IS NOT EXCLUSIONARY

I want to continue the thinking above but take it in a different direction. Unless you are a terminally evil person, there is nothing about who you are that disqualifies you from being a good manager. There is no personality type that must be present for you to be effective as a manager. Your personality type definitely shapes how you will manage people, but you can be effective in that role with many different styles.

This is a very important point, and here's another way to see it. There are very specific management jobs that will exclude the vast majority of the population, but for every management-ready individual, there is some management role they can fill. For instance, managing an NFL team will require someone who is not afraid of conflict as they shape the effort of huge egos and strong-willed stakeholders (owners, fans, media, etc.). That's just part of the job, and putting a conflict-averse manager in there is a sure recipe for failure. But managing a classroom of special needs children doesn't require that so much as it requires empathy and patience. If we swapped roles between these two people, they both would fail, not because they aren't good managers but because the specific requirements of that management role weren't taken into account when managers were considered.

What this means is that some managers fail because of the fit and not because of their aptitude. It also means that in the right circumstance, a good person—no matter the personality traits—can manage well if attention is paid to that fit.

MANAGEMENT DOES NOT MAKE YOU SPECIAL

There's a strange hierarchy built into the socio-economic structure of the "developed" world. If you want to make a lot of money, you either have to be one of the lucky few entertainers or athletes inexplicably lauded by the unwashed masses, or you have to manage people. Left out of this mix is the craft or skill person who accepts a management job because of the money and prestige that comes with it, never mind that they are a terrible fit.

What this heading should have said, really, is this: Being a Manager Will Make You and Others Think You Are Special, but You Really Aren't. What I'm saying is that management should be viewed as a job. That is, it's a job that involves stepping out of the details, looking at trends, acting like a coach, and all the other things that come with it. But that's not necessarily more important than what the people on your team do, and you need to disabuse yourself of that idea or you'll be haughty and unapproachable.

If I could wave a magic wand, there would be two career paths—one for skill/craft and one for management—and given individuals could move up each path without crossing over to the other. In that world, some skill/craft employees would be making more money than the managers who are responsible for them. Who cares? This notion that money moves in lock-step with your ascent on the corporate ladder has left us with a lot of idiots doing what they think is management only because that comes with the higher salary and they can't ignore it entirely. If you can't manage people well, you shouldn't be a manager. It's that simple, really. And you could even extrapolate that and say that if you can't manage people, you don't have any business owning a company that employs them.

THE TITLE MUST FLOW FROM THE ACTIVITY

When you think about it, I believe you'll agree that there should be no surprises in management. Kudos, disciplinary actions, promotions, demotions, labor contraction. All these things should be largely expected when they happen (except perhaps to the clueless crowd).

Looking more specifically into promotions, ask yourself this: when the people who work around you found out that you were being promoted to a manager, did they scratch their heads and say: "Wow. I wonder where that came from. What an odd choice." Or did they nod their heads and note the decision, even just in passing, as one that made sense.

You're always aiming for the latter. Great managers are generally great managers before they ever have the title. They're like an inner tube you're trying to hide from your brother by submerging it. Eventually, you get tired of holding it down and the inner tube (or the truth, in this case) pops to the surface.

Managers manage. Leaders lead. It generally happens or it doesn't, and the title is almost immaterial. If you're promoted to management for the right reasons, you're already doing it, even if you don't recognize it.

This is all really good news for most of you, because it means that all you have to do now is maintain the same direction, learn the formal parts of what is expected of you, avoid the land mines, and not let your head get too big. (I'm going to help you with that last part in this book.)

PEOPLE MUST KNOW YOU ARE MANAGING THEM

Similar to the idea that there are few surprises in management decisions, there are absolutely no secrets when it comes to who people are reporting to. There may very well be significant confusion about it, but there are no secrets. If people don't know you are managing them, well, then you aren't managing them. Period.

I've asked more than 8,000 people to name their boss. That's always struck me as a pretty simple question, right? You'd probably agree with that. They do, too, until they have to answer it.

Most people give me an immediate answer, and they identify one person by name. This indicates that there is a clear reporting structure in that particular management environment.

Others pause, think a little, and then finally give me a name, and that's a sure indication of some problem in the environment. Listen, asking someone to identify their boss is a lot like asking them who their Dad is. Either you know or you don't, and there shouldn't be much delay between the question and the answer.

Worse yet is the person who pauses, and then names several people. That's no good, folks. What it generally means is that no one is managing them at all.

So here's the point: someone cannot promote you to a management role and keep it a secret. Either you are officially managing people or you aren't, and if you are, they must know that you are. When someone tries to promote you to a management role but doesn't want the people "below" you to know that, there's a very good chance that what they are really doing is making you responsible for the results without giving you the authority to shape them.

As Dr. Phil would say, "Let me know how that works out."

THERE IS NO OFFICIAL MANAGEMENT WITHOUT POWER

That leads us to the final point of this section, and that's the relationship between your management role and the power that comes with that role. The essence of management certainly isn't power, at least wielded power. It's more about influence, which in itself is power, but it's more the ability to instill in people a legitimate desire to follow your leadership.

Real management, then, is about how you act and what you say and what you ignore and how you treat people and all those other things that we're going to talk about. But as critical as all those things are, and as well as you might handle them, you really aren't managing people in the truest sense of the word unless these things are largely true of your role.

First, you are responsible for hiring the people you manage, even if the decision must be approved by someone else. Or at least you are a significant part of the approval loop.

Second, you make the decisions or at least the recommendations for the compensation of the people you manage.

Third, if the people you manage receive performance reviews, you are the person who gives them, and if someone else attends the performance reviews, they are there merely as a silent witness.

Fourth, you have the authority to dismiss someone you manage, even if the decision must be approved by someone else.

Be sure to look a little deeper under the title you've just been given to see if it's really management or not. If these things aren't true of your new role, you ain't managing, baby. And if that's just now become apparent to you, put the book down and ask for a clarifying conversation with the person who promoted you and don't proceed until you know what you're getting into.

When you're ready, the next thing we're going to do is take a deeper look at why you were promoted. Understanding that will help you understand the things that happen early in your career as a new manager.

2

Was I Promoted
For The Right Reasons

I'll never forget joining the Rotary Club in our little town, years ago. I was surprised at how soon afterwards I was asked to be one of the greeters. I also thought that at the time that it was a pretty good way to match names with faces, and figured that this was the primary reason.

Four years later I was president of that large club, and it dawned on me that what they asked me to do that day wasn't be a greeter but to begin a four-year program to being president. It wasn't that they saw something in me that made me a great candidate for president; it was more that they found a sucker who was willing to help and who didn't see the president thing coming!

Was I promoted for the wrong reasons? Not really. All they were testing at that point was my willingness to help. If I passed that test, and if they later saw leadership qualities in me, they'd keep moving me from one position to the next. It was a proven, logical way to move someone into a management position. Oh that things worked that way in the typical small business, where we had a written advancement plan with key stepping stones and support along the way. Not so, unfortunately.

THE WAY IT USUALLY HAPPENS

In the real world that's more reactive than we'd all like, here's how it usually unfolds.

First, opportunity comes along that the entrepreneurial owner can't resist. Saying "no" is so painful that it's just not seriously considered. Instead of saying "no" and preserving that gap between opportunity and capacity (the very gap that gives you all the power in client relationships), capacity is increased to match opportunity and the body count goes up. The new recruits filter in, they're given a hasty orientation, and dropped behind enemy lines.

Second, things get a little crazy. The key people at the place were overworked before the new people were added, so imagine what it's like now. The added people are justifying higher work volumes, which means tighter bottlenecks, more things to track, and an increasingly deeper exasperation with how unsustainable this is, especially for the people who are the bottlenecks.

Third, the higher ups are reluctantly dragged, kicking and screaming, to the realization that a new layer between them and the worker bees is necessary. They typically started the business based on some valued technical expertise, and so this is not an easy decision. As exciting as the opportunity is that has forced this growth (in their minds), there's a great reluctance at removing themselves from the daily work that they are good at, that they enjoy, and that has presumably brought the firm to its present successful place.

Fourth, they have to make a decision on who is going to serve in this layer. The obvious two choices are a promotion from within or a hire from without. Promotion from within isn't usually the exciting option, though it's viewed as the safer one since you know what you're getting. But it's not exciting because there's nothing new being brought to the table. Instead, you typically end up with someone who will maintain the status quo, keep things on an even keel, and keep doing things the way the departing owner/manager has wanted them to be done.

An outside hire is more exciting, and could obviously teach the firm a thing or two, but it's risky. It's also time consuming, and time is one thing we don't have. Oh, and it's quite a bit more expensive. Not just because of the higher compensation they'll likely require, but all the search fees, moving expenses, and signing bonuses.

But as true as all that is, it's not really what tips the scale between promotion or hiring. What it really comes down to is perception issues. Namely, how will it strike those in the department if an outsider is brought in instead of promoting someone from within? Will they resent it? Will they keep working as hard if they think their chances of advancement are not as great as they thought before? In other words, how will existing employees view their own career paths if, when future promotions are possible, the company just goes outside the firm again to hire for significant positions?

Fifth, they choose you. I'm pretty comfortable assuming that your first job managing people came from an internal promotion and not from a lateral move between companies. It's very rare for a new employer to take that sort of chance—it's one thing to take a chance on hiring you, but it's much riskier to take a chance that involves other people, too (those you would manage).

But why did they choose to promote you? That's the crux of this chapter, and we need to look very closely at that because the answer will provide all sorts of clues to what your (early) management experience will be like.

Now picture the person above you who has already decided that he or she is going to promote from within, at least this first time. Whatever their reasons, good or bad, that's the decision. So at this point all outside alternatives are eliminated and it's a choice between all the people already working in the department. As they look out and survey all those folks, what criteria do they use to make that choice?

HOW INTERNAL PROMOTIONS ARE OFTEN MADE

In watching this process unfold a hundred times in all sorts of firms, I've seen some interesting patterns emerge. All these patterns won't be present in every situation, but you'll quickly spot the ones that might be present in yours.

One essential note, too, before explaining the way promotions are usually made. In each of the following three points, I'm going to describe the action that an average manager would take. (I'm talking about the manager above you; the one who is promoting you. The best managers don't do these things, but the best managers, by definition, are not all that common.)

First, average managers tend to find someone to take over the role they have been playing and do things the same way. The new manager doesn't rock the boat, doesn't try to "improve" things all that much, and doesn't try to reinvent the wheel. I've identified this hiring supervisor as average because often you'll find that they have significant control freak tendencies, and they are looking for a replacement like them. Does this describe your situation? If it does, and if you think highly of the way things are being done, you probably have nothing to fear. But if you intend to change things, be prepared to accept the risk that comes with experimentation.

The best managers hire people (like you, hopefully) who can step into a role and do something better than the way it's been done before. They have something to teach the company so that it moves beyond the competency level of the current managers.

This is why it often makes sense for you to move to another company after you get this first management stint under your belt. The new company doesn't have you in a box, and you may be perceived as an outside expert that the new company you move to can learn from. This isn't always true, but it's something to consider.

Second, average managers are very worried about what people think, and so when they look across the group as they try to choose the employee to succeed them, they inevitably land on the best producer. Not because that person is the best manager to take his or her place, but because they don't want to anger the best producer to the point where they quit producing.

Here's the problem with that, though. Being the best producer has absolutely nothing to do with being a good manager. And here we get to the heart of this chapter: were you promoted because you were the best producer or because you showed the promise of being the best manager. It's not that one excludes the other, because you might have been chosen for this management position because you were the best producer, but that doesn't mean you won't grow into a great manager. "It could happen," as they say—it's just that there's no connection between the two.

What we've arrived at here is one of the fundamental flaws in how things typically happen.

"I need less contact with the front lines because the business as a whole is suffering and because I'm burning out in a role that's very unsustainable. I could hire someone from the outside to create this new layer, or I could move someone up from the inside. That'll probably go over better, so I'll do that. But who? Well, Candice is my best producer, by far, and I can't afford to lose her. And she's not likely to accept having Jim over her, even though I suspect Jim might be a better manager. So I guess I'll give it to Candice and hope that she grows into this role. But she must keep producing, because the department's output would look very different without her still doing our best work."

Can you see all the compromises in that way of thinking? If you were just promoted by an exceptional manager, that person chose you because you showed management ability already, along with at least enough technical competence to earn the respect of your former peers who will now answer to you. This puts you on an easier path.

If, however, you were promoted because you were the best producer, well, you have some interesting times ahead of you. You'll face the pressure of maintaining a high output level while you try to figure out how to handle the additional responsibilities that come with your promotion. You'll be guiding performance, building a team, maintaining communication, mentoring the slower learners, and so on.

Are you excited about this? Or at least eager to accept the challenge? If you were promoted for the wrong reasons and if you are not up to this challenge, put this book down and go rescind the promotion. I'm as serious as I can be about that.

Accepting a management role (for the first time) because of the additional prestige and money that comes with it will make you more miserable than you can imagine. Worse yet, it'll make those below you—and above you—just as miserable. Those below you will be screaming for your management and leadership while you have your head down, "producing" stuff night and day, primarily because that's a comfortable place for you. There will be a slow, sinking disintegration around you and eventually you'll be run out of the place.

Again, the best managers unbundle technical expertise from management aptitude, and they make the right decisions on both fronts. We're going to expand on that in this next point. For now, make sure that's the sort of person who has promoted you.

Third, average managers think that respect comes primarily from technical expertise. This is something we touched on in the second point above, but it cannot get lost without being singled out as its own point. Consider this for a minute: some of the largest, most successful companies in the world are led by people who don't know how to do the actual work as well as thousands of other people below him or her who know how to do it better. Then ask yourself why this is, and you'll realize that it's because this forces them to manage, bypassing the temptation to step and "fix" something themselves.

That is such a key point that if it wouldn't look tacky, I'd splash that one single statement all by itself on this page. A great manager does not have to have the strongest technical understanding of what the people he or she manages do for a living. (All over the world right now you can hear sighs of relief from managers who are so grateful that this is true or they'd be screwed.)

A great manager who might promote you that first time understands that you might very well need enough technical understanding that people listen to you. But they also might realize that what makes you a great candidate for this new position is who you are, not what you know.

So forget this fear you may have about whether you "know" enough to lead these people who just yesterday were peers. Sure, the more you know, the more you might feel comfortable, but if you were chosen for the right reasons, that is not why you were chosen.

REVIEW

Step back for a minute, now, and ask yourself some questions.

Have I largely demonstrated the right choices in the recent past, and is that why I've been given this promotion?

Do I understand that this is not primarily about prestige and higher pay, but about being responsible for the performance, output, and growth of other employees in a business setting?

Have I already been managing people even if I didn't yet have the title or the official power that goes with it?

As this transition has been explained to me, will my new management role be explained as such, publicly, so that others will know that I am their new boss without any hedging or grayness?

Will I have the appropriate power with this title?

Will it be okay if I put my own stamp on how this group of people does effective work?

Was I chosen for the right reasons?

If you are comfortable with your answers to those questions, you're on the right path and it's time to start down this path on the right foot. That's what we're going to look at next.

3

Starting Off Right

If you've ever tiled a floor, you know how important it is to have the right start. If the first row of tiles is off even just a little, the mistake is magnified with each subsequent row. The same is true of a journey. Imagine taking off from New York City and following a heading that's only two degrees to the right. When you started looking around for the airport in San Francisco, you'd be far north of there.

Sure, you can make course adjustments along the way, but when you start out managing from the wrong place, it's more like having to tear the tile floor up and rebuild it than simply moving the yoke in the cockpit—the consequences of starting off on the wrong foot in a management environment involve wasted time, wasted money, and a possible job move so that you can start over. So let's not do that.

The first thing to take into account when starting out is that your promotion will be polarizing. Your supporters will be invigorated and love you even more than they did before. In most cases that's a good thing because they have loved you for the right reasons in the first place. But as you can guess, some of them loved you for their own selfish reasons and they think that by supporting the right candidate in the primary, so to speak, they're now in a position to ask for a reward for their loyalty. They're comfortable with advancing on merit, but with a sly wink they whisper that it's always helpful to have good friends in high places.

But as I said, most of the people who have been your supporters will have done so for the right reasons, and your recent promotion will warm their hearts.

Your detractors, however, will be a different story. They'll be even more firm in their stance against you, though they'll take it underground. How do you win these folks over?

Don't overreact in attempting to win over your detractors—the peers who would have rather seen someone else promoted to your new position. Here are some specific thoughts on how to handle dissent in the early days of a promotion.

First, acknowledge it. Address it directly without equivocation. You might have a conversation like this. "Thanks for a few minutes of your time. I would guess that my promotion may be a difficult one for you, and that if you had been making the choice, I would not have been your first choice. I just wanted to acknowledge that between us, not to change your mind about it, but to encourage as much open communication between us as possible. You're a valuable resource here [only say that if it's true] and I think we can help each other. I'm going to do my best to be a good leader, and I hope my definition of that is one that you end up being comfortable with. I don't want to make all sorts of promises or build a false sense of teamwork, though. Instead, I'd rather just do my job well and let you determine on your own if I'm doing a good job or not. I appreciate having different points of view around me, and I hope you'll be comfortable sharing yours with me when you think we could do something better." Whatever you say should be true, but you don't need to say everything you know. Be kind, gracious, and patient.

Second, don't give detractors too much power. You can do that by worrying too much about their impact, making rash promises/alliances, coddling them with reactions that are too softened, and just listening too much. The only thing worse than an unfair detractor is a detractor that is emboldened by early success.

Third, don't insult detractors by patronizing them. You should be genuinely open to their perspective, but you should accord it the proper weight. Whatever interaction you have with them should be sincere and not meant primarily to engender some reaction in them. In other words, don't ask for their feedback unless you want it. The truth about your management style is not something to be feared. Instead, let it wash over you and just try to be a better manager. Where that truth comes from is not really all that important. If it comes from an overreacting detractor, well, just pull out the truth and pitch the rest. If you fear being misunderstood, well, buck up and welcome to management.

Fourth, concentrate on doing the right thing and let the chips fall where they may. We'll look at this in great depth later.

REMEMBERING THE LARGER CONTEXT

As you start out on this adventure, it'll be important to remember several things. Your attitude and actions should at a minimum take the larger context into account, and you may have to go beyond that and actually address the context.

For example, why were you chosen for this position? We've discussed this at length above, but if you were chosen for the wrong reason, then obviously there will be issues. If you were chosen for the right reasons but others don't agree with that, there will be other issues to deal with.

What caused this watershed event? Did they make a bad hire with the person just before you, and are now making the safe (if uninspired) choice? Was your predecessor accurate in his or her assessment, but maybe too provocative in the presentation of it? Were they fired, with little explanation, and many of the employees are still distracted because they can't understand why?

It's even possible that you'll need to lay low for a bit, especially if the event that created this opportunity for you is bigger than the opportunity itself, at least in the minds of those in your care. This category might include an egregious violation of a non-compete, misappropriation of company property, sexual harassment, or substance abuse.

This promotion will undoubtedly be a significant milestone in your life, but others may see it in a very different context. The pacing of your "taking charge" and making significant pronouncements must take that into account. Some situations would call for aggressive planning, significant pronouncements, and major rollouts with a flurry of activity, all designed to give people the comfort that you are in charge, finally, and the ship is no longer rudderless.

Other settings would appropriately bring careful planning, a lot of work behind the scenes, and individual meetings to build a support base. This is more likely to convince those who are weary of leadership pronouncements without follow through. They're skeptical and disengaged.

So, read the room and start out appropriately so that you don't lose your audience early in the process.

FIRST IMPRESSIONS

I would suggest that you keep a log of your first impressions, from the very first day this unfolds (or even before that, as the discussions of your role take place). There are two important reasons for this.

First, you'll find it very interesting to refer back to this later, when you are fully entrenched in the management role but hit some snag. It might provide some perspective on how things have changed in the larger picture, or it might give you some insight on the seeds to this particular struggle.

Second, you never know when you may be called up to mentor or coach or train a newer manager. These notes can serve as a useful prod in bringing some of those memories to the surface.

ACCEPTANCE SPEECH

Okay, it's really not an acceptance speech in the traditional sense, but the first public discussion of your new role really ought to set the tone. What you say and how you say it can play all the right notes, or—if you bungle it—you'll spend the next six months undoing the damage caused by an unfortunate choice of words or a badly timed joke.

During management transitions, here is what people are looking for from you.

First, they want you and not some version of what you think "you" should be. Your charges can smell lack of authenticity like burning hair on a forearm. There's just no mistaking it, no hiding it, and no covering it up. All you've really got is you, and if that's not enough, well...then you have another problem that a book like this is never going to fix. Don't wrap some "management tone" around your voice, or walk differently, or communicate some "apartness" that separates you from them. You aren't all that special, frankly, and really you're the same person you were before you were promoted. Be human.

Second, they want to see your confidence. They don't expect you to be right all the time but they don't want to see you hesitate before every move. They want to see you make considered decisions, but in the end they do want you to make decisions. This confidence doesn't come from dismissing all external input, but from knowing how much weight to give it and when to make a digital decision in an world that will always remain analog.

They want you to be collaborative. Not too collaborative, where everyone holds equal sway, but collaborative because of an understanding that the people in the trenches usually do have the answers and are thus genuinely worth listening to. Ask them—if you really mean it—to participate in a self-assessment of what could be done differently to maximize our potential together. But don't do that unless you're going to listen or they'll resent it.

They want you to be engaged, which is a better term than "eager." They are looking to see if this matters to you and if doing this work will yield some sense of accomplishment in your mind. People want to be a part of something bigger. In the end, a job is about the money, but if there isn't more to it than that, the feeling is hollow and not terribly self-fulfilling.

They want you to chart a direction for the department with just enough detail that they can see the outline of a goal against the fog of the future, but without so much detail that it looks like you need their acceptance of every little component. Ultimately, they want to know that the many seemingly inconsequential decisions you make in a day are governed by a larger plan with some intention behind it.

They want, finally, for you to be hopeful, which is not the same as positive. Positive people are generally in denial. Hopeful people are facing the challenges and still moving forward eagerly.

4
Managing Your Boss

The idea of managing your boss is meant to be a bit tongue in cheek, but the concept is real and the extent to which you accomplish this is directly related to the extent of your positive impact as a manager.

So let's look briefly at a few important aspects of managing your boss, recognizing that your management efforts are not directed just downward, but also upward.

WHY YOU WERE PROMOTED

We've talked about this extensively already, so there's no sense in repeating it here. Suffice it to say that you must write this down in a private place, recognizing that you can't really ask the question directly. So divine the answer as best you can.

So let me summarize the various possible reasons for your promotion by listing the four most common ones I observe. Choose between them and note the primary reason, perhaps also noting a secondary reason.

The first possible reason for your promotion was to keep you from leaving. Your new boss both recognized your significant skill (largely in the sense of a craft or specific training), and they didn't want to lose you through the process of promoting someone to a management role. They feared that promoting someone else would cause you to leave, and that was a result they feared.

The second possible reason for your promotion was to improve the technical problems in the department. Which is quite different than managing others who will then fix those technical problems. The distinction here is your personal, hands-on expertise versus your skill in managing other experts.

The third possible reason for your promotion was to continue the same management path that your current boss established. In this role you're viewed more as a caretaker or babysitter, continuing the traditions that someone else before you established. This is about doing what someone else already thinks is best with minimal disruption or questioning.

The fourth possible reason for your promotion was to acknowledge and take advantage of your management and leadership skills. This is obviously the ideal reason, and the one we are assuming to be true.

PREFERRED COMMUNICATION METHODS

Everybody has certain preferences about how communication happens. If this concept is a mystery to you, it might be best to have you and your boss take the same personality profile to surface these in a more scientific manner. Or, you can simply bring your powers of observation to bear and note the patterns that surface.

Ask yourself first if your boss wants to be kept tightly in the loop at every stage of any difficulty as it unfolds, or if they would rather you manage these problems on your own and then provide a debriefing when the issue has passed. Certain bosses want no surprises; others want no clutter; and some prefer something between these two extremes.

If your boss is the type that wants no surprises, they had better hear of an issue first from you or they'll not have the confidence to rely on your initiative. Instead, they'll always be wondering what's just under the surface that you haven't informed them about yet.

At the other extreme would be the boss who is more likely to state something like this: "Don't bring me a problem without the solution." This is someone looking to not be bothered. They feel like they have enough problems of their own (at a higher level), and they don't look favorably at the opportunity to mentor or coach you. To them, management is a never-ending stream of problems to be solved, and like a bug on a windshield: wipe it off and move on. They'll be eager to give you credit for solving an issue without their involvement, but they'll be eager to blame you for not handling something, too, which they would define as having to get personally involved to clean up the mess that your mop wasn't big enough to take care of. So think of this as primarily about the frequency and timing of your communication upward.

The second thing to ask yourself about your boss' preferred communication style is the method itself. Do they prefer email, phone, or in person? Someone who prefers email is usually bent toward the more efficient, less relational style. They want the data, primarily. Others might prefer a method where they can assess the tone of the exchange, or perhaps even think out loud. Their thoughts are formed in the articulation itself. Or maybe they want an answer now, and a phone call or meeting requires a two-way exchange in which both parties are engaged at the same time. An in-person meeting might even be a power move where you are summoned to someone else's turf where the power structure is clearer.

Your boss will use various methods at various times, but be sure you're aware of their normal propensities, and try to understand why those methods work for him or her. Being someone your boss enjoys managing isn't about you always being the comfortable party. At times it means that you are the more self-aware individual in this relationship and that you intentionally act in ways that will provide fewer distractions to your boss. That's simply maturity on your part.

The third thing to consider in managing your boss is the timing of your communication, specifically in three categories: day, week, and month.

For the first, is your boss a morning person, or do they become more engaged as the day unfolds? This has everything to do with how they'll absorb and react to those issues that must be addressed. You don't really have a choice in addressing them or not, but you can certainly choose when to address them, and making the right choice in this regard will facilitate your management relationship.

For the second, is there a pattern in how your boss' life unfolds during a typical week? Does she have a management check-in with her boss on Monday, often leaving her dispirited? That's not the time to expect the best exchange with her. When are the things on her plate categorized and delegated, freeing her from as many distractions as possible? If you aren't going to benefit from a manager's full attention, it's better to wait for a time when you can.

For the third, look for a similar pattern in how the month unfolds for your boss. Is the end of the month full of unusual pressure while chasing sales goals and final reports? Or is the first part of the month the most challenging as she establishes new initiatives and sets new paths?

Pay attention to what your boss is facing so that over time she looks forward to exchanges with you. If, however, she learns to dread those exchanges, then she'll learn to dread you as a manager. The how and when of an exchange is just as important as the what. This will be clearer to you as a manager as the individual employees in your charge manage the process well, or not so well.

EXPECTATIONS

Recently I was conducting a seminar with eighty managers, many of whom managed sister departments on an equal footing at the same company. I asked each of the managers to imagine hiring a well-qualified employee for a specific function, picture a very well executed orientation program on their behalf, and then answer one question: how many weeks would they expect to pass before this well-qualified, well-integrated employee is fully contributing in their new role.

My question was meant to surface the expectations that these fellow-managers had within the same company. Was that new employee expected to be at full-impact immediately? After four weeks? Maybe six months?

Each manager had to write their answer down to avoid influence from another manager, and then I asked them to read their responses as we worked our way through the room, table to table.

The varying responses were a shock to me, ranging from "I'd expect them to be at full-impact immediately" to "I wouldn't expect them to be at full-impact until they'd worked here for about one year."

That got me to thinking that any new manager better find out what sort of expectation a boss might have, right? If I'm in your shoes and I give myself three months to really get up to speed, but my supervisor thinks I should be up to speed within two weeks, we're going to have a significant disconnect.

And significant disconnects come primarily from lack of clear, concise communication. So come right out and ask your boss what their expectations are. "As you think about the relative complexity of this role, the recent history of our department, and my capabilities, what is your expectation of the time required for me to get up to speed and contribute fully? How many weeks or months do you have in mind? I'm asking simply to be as clear as I can be about your expectations of me."

Once you have your answer, memorialize it in some way. If this takes place as a conversation, send a summary email to your boss, ostensibly so that they know that you have understood the mandate, but also so that you'll have a record of their expectation should their memory of it fade in the future. So that's the first thing: find out how much time you have.

The second thing you'll want to know is how your boss is going to measure success. Be very specific about this. Will it be measured in terms of staff utilization? Carefully managed make-dos? Employee turnover? The number of problems that are delegated upward? The hours you work?

This won't be a simple answer, and if you think your boss believes it's a simple answer, you must probe deeper. Find out very specifically how success will be measured and then (if you agree at a basic level with their perspective) be sure that you don't neglect that aspect of all that's on your plate. Again, it's about communication. You can't be expected to know what someone else is thinking, much less meet a goal you aren't even aware of. So request specific goals against which you will be measured. And be prepared to discover that your boss hasn't even thought about it that specifically. If that's the case, give them fair warning so that they can give it careful consideration. The best bosses welcome an opportunity to articulate their expectations, and they'll be grateful that you want to know what they are. Just don't embarrass anybody by springing the question on them without warning.

MANAGEMENT COMMITMENT TO YOU

The last major category of managing your boss has to do with determining the level of their management commitment to you. Though it probably goes without saying, you won't need to do any of these things if you have a great boss. They might define their own management commitment to you differently than I'm going to define it, but there will be no mistaking it. You will know for sure that they are one of those ideal bosses—flawed, but self-aware, and committed to the right things.

Other than that very small group of just plain evil bosses you might have inherited, the vast majority of bosses mean well but just have trouble making it happen. There are so many competing demands for their time that they attend to emergencies, first. And since (presumably) you are a good employee and not an emergency, you might be neglected a bit. That might hurt your feelings, but it's not really prudent to jump to that conclusion. You might even consider it an honor!

Nevertheless, you have a legitimate need and right to prompt your manager for a certain kind of interaction with you, and I'm going to make two suggestions about making that happen.

The first suggestion is to make the twenty-minute walks we'll describe later (the ones between you and those you manage) also occur between you and your boss. We don't need to get into that here, but when you read that section, don't just think of what you should be doing with those in your management care, but also think about making that happen with your boss.

The second suggestion is to seek candor from your boss. There's no way for me to know how candid your boss is, of course. I've seen the silent angry type, the passive-aggressive manipulator behind the scenes, the boss who is terrified of conflict, the nit picking control freak boss, and the boss who somehow broaches tough subjects without any sense of attacking you. Regardless of how your specific boss interacts with you, accept the responsibility to probe deeper, read between the lines, draw them out, and in general make sure you leave a conversation knowing for sure what they believe. It doesn't matter so much if you agree with it, but it is impossible to really improve your relationship with the boss unless you can determine what they really believe about your performance.

So drop the anger or martyr role and strive for clear communication. The more you make it easier for your boss to be candid with you, the better the relationship will be. Who knows. Maybe you're the person who will be the tipping point for your boss. Later, they'll look back and say that they learned more about management from managing you than any other experience they've previously encountered. Take up that challenge, be humble, be open to what they have to say, and try to put yourself in their place, with all the past history and current pressures. Be somebody that they compare others to, wishing that the other people they managed were like you.

If your boss really is an idiot, though, don't spend much extra time worrying about what that person thinks.

FINALLY

When you get further down the road of managing others, there will be a time when you find yourself being extremely grateful for those few employees in your management care who have what I call the "conversational fairness" trait. As you experience this, you know that conversations about you and your management style are taking place apart from your presence, but when that happens, you know that this person with "conversational fairness" is just that: fair in conversations where you are not present.

These folks are not easily swayed by what others think, and they don't say one thing when you aren't listening and another when you are. When speaking privately with others about you, they openly disagree with stands you have taken when that's called for, and they defend you when that's appropriate. Either way, they have a considered point of view and don't "pile on" when others are being unfair.

So, here's my question for you. Are you that same sort of person when talking about your boss? If you are, the truth is more important to you than being liked, and that's going to be a very useful foundational trait as you manage other people.

5

Early Discoveries

Hopefully we've got you in your new job, now, all settled in and ready to hit the ground running. You're likely brimming with optimism, albeit tinged with a bit of apprehension. What's coming next? What are you about to discover that might be a little surprising? Let's look at five typical realizations that you'll make early on along this path.

BEING MISUNDERSTOOD

The first early discovery you'll make is that some of your earlier commentary as an employee (not a manager) was unfair whining. Like all employees do, you gave your opinion about management decisions without really knowing all the facts (which will always be true) and without making allowances for that gap in knowledge. You failed to give earlier managers along your career path the same sort of benefit of the doubt that you now crave, and that realization is hitting you right between the eyes. Now you understand what it means to be misunderstood. You realize that it's painful, and you also understand the temptation to "pull" on the employees in your care by sounding them out, accepting artificial consensus, and gravitating toward those who are more open in their public support.

If we flip this around, you'll always need to make allowances for employee comments that indicate a misunderstanding of what's really going on. There's no way to eliminate this and you'll just have to accept it. That means, among other things, that you'll need to construct your emotional well-being around the assumption that even the best managers in the world are managing employees who say unfair things. If your emotional health depends on being understood, well, it's going to be a pretty disappointing experience. You'll have to learn to operate in an environment where misunderstanding is always felt and acknowledged but not so distracting that you lose focus.

As I've told thousands of business owners over the years, "there are cheaper ways to make friends." By that I mean that by unduly shaping your decisions to achieve the goal of making everybody like you is going to make artificial friends, and expensive artificial friends at that! To look at just one example, imagine what sort of discussions you'll have around salary issues if your goal is to make people happy and/or to get them to say nice things about you in private.

So be prepared for misunderstanding and unfairness. It's inevitable and will not serve as a reliable indicator of some failure on your part.

Before we leave this topic, though, let me add one important caveat. The extent to which employees misunderstand you could certainly indicate some failure to manage well, but the existence of it does not. That's a very complicated way of saying that good managers will always be misunderstood, but that should not be used as a license to accept misunderstanding. You can't turn all this around and say "all these employees are wrong about me. Even the best managers are misunderstood."

This is something you have to watch carefully. Be cautious in evaluating the extent of the misunderstanding you sense. If most of the employees "misunderstand" you, that's a sure sign that you're the problem and not them. And in the end it's really not a "misunderstanding" but an "understanding." They get it and you don't.

Deliberate well, make the right decisions, live with some misunderstanding, recognize that the truth always surfaces (eventually), and be prepared to be wrong.

FACING LONELINESS

The second early discovery you'll make—and one that is closely related to the first discovery—is that management can be lonely. If you don't struggle with some loneliness, you probably are doing something wrong. Any leadership position is lonely, whether that's managing a department, owning a company, being a parent, or serving in elected office. (And I speak from experience in all four categories.) A fundamental human need is to be understood by several people, and the loneliness of your new position stems from being misunderstood by the people you rub shoulders with every day.

To feel that loneliness, you have to be doing several things. The first is making decisions. The second is observing the impact of those decisions. The third is being sufficiently honest and self-aware to freely admit that loneliness. So you can see how some loneliness is actually a good sign—all three of these things are exactly what you should be doing. Loneliness can very well indicate that you're doing the right things. But too much loneliness, or responding to the loneliness in inappropriate ways, indicates the opposite. If you're overwhelmed with loneliness (absent some other emotional issue unrelated to your management duties), you care way too much about whether or not these employees in your care will accept you, and the end result is that you'll be a lousy leader.

What are the best ways of responding to this loneliness? I want to make three specific suggestions.

I'd urge you first to have an exciting, stimulating life of learning and curiosity and interesting hobbies outside of your role at work. The more overlap that exists between your work and your personal life, the stranger the demands you'll place on work. That's because it'll have to be much more than work to fill those personal voids, and when you depend on work to do it, you begin to justify all sorts of strange decisions along the way. More on this in a later chapter.

Next, I'd urge you to make some very good friends with your peers, both within the company and at a similar level at other companies. There's no need to reinvent the wheel, here, and there's much to learn from others. If nothing else, finding that others are working through the same issues will be some relief, assuring you that God isn't singling you out to be Job II.

Finally, take advantage of a strong support system of family, mentors, associations, and friends. Preferably, lean the most on people who believe in you but who will also be honest with you. Belief without honesty is cheerleading. Honesty without belief is just cruelty.

DOING VS. MANAGING

The third early discovery you'll make is that there is virtually no connection between "doing" and "managing" something. Michael Gerber impacted many entrepreneurs when he wrote about the "E-Myth," or the myth that there really aren't any entrepreneurs. Instead, he said, most people start out as technicians and then somehow come to the belief that knowing how to "do" something is not all that different from knowing how to "manage" the people who will "do" that thing.

There's virtually no overlap. In fact, some of the most successful companies on the planet are run by people who don't know how to do the work. How can that be? It's simple, really: without the temptation to step in all the time—simply because they don't know how to do the work that needs fixed—they have no choice but to build a strong team that will do the work. So they hire well, onboard well, train well, manage well, and the net result is an expert manager who is managing a group of valued experts.

This may very well be the most misunderstood aspect of management. As we noted above, misunderstandings in this area lead to bad promotion decisions. Too often the best doers are the ones promoted, and these doers may have no interest in managing others and simply "do" to avoid the proper management role. From there, it extends to who the new manager hires, which ends up being younger doers who can be taught the same methods or who are hired merely to help the manager who isn't managing because there's so much doing.

Listen, if you think your greatest value is being the "Super Doer," you're not really going to build a team; you won't spread the praise around; the department will be crippled whenever you aren't there; it'll be hard to attract great employees because they aren't given a chance to blossom; and so on. I could give you another dozen results from too much doing, but you've likely witnessed this first hand.

Here's a foundational truth, folks. Every increase in body count requires adaptation in the manage/do mix at the top. In my observation over the years, all the doing typically gets squeezed out of a job description when those directly in your care number somewhere between ten and twenty. Beyond that, it'll take an actual or pseudo layer of management help to shape people's performance appropriately. So the more you insist on doing, the less time you'll have to manage.

Sure, stepping in and helping with the actual work is necessary from time to time, but this should get more difficult for you. First, you ought to be out of practice, which means that you'll struggle getting up to speed when something needs to be solved. In these cases your greatest value is in guiding the knowledge of others through a problem-solving exercise instead of solving the problem with your own knowledge. The second reason these forays should be difficult for you is this: if you're doing your job right, you should be hiring experts, and experts are people who can teach you things, not people who need to learn things from you. Yes, they need to learn about management and communication and they need to learn all sorts of things, really, but they shouldn't need to learn technical expertise from you.

So do you want to do or manage? The answer to that question, my friend, is going to have a meteor-like impact on your own impact. It's not like you'll only have to ask yourself this question once, either, right at the outset of your transition to management. The question will keep coming up, over and over, and it'll be a long time before your natural instincts are retrained.

You're now the fire chief, okay? While on-site, monitoring a blaze, the best use of your skills is to shape the expertise of others. If you insist on rescuing everybody yourself, none of the firefighters are going to want to work for you anymore. They'll admire you at first, but then they'll start making jokes about the "cowboy firefighter" who fashions himself as God's gift to firefighting. If your antics continue, eventually they'll quit dressing in the appropriate gear and just pull up a lawn chair and watch you bust your butt. Then they'll just quit coming altogether.

Your job is to serve your employees. Their job is to serve your customers.

If you don't get that fundamental principle right, you'll find yourself serving your customers directly, and it's too darn big of a job for you to do it well.

What all this points to is really the source of your satisfaction. Up until this point, a large portion of it has come from customer kudos, and maybe even kudos from previous managers. The "job well done" has been quite measurable and immediately satisfying. But all that has changed. Your new job is not that measurable or even visible. It's a quiet, steady, do-the-right-thing sort of job. It's helping others succeed, and somehow learning to find a real contentment in an approach that's more service-oriented and behind the scenes.

But remember how this book started? I asked you to think about the fact that the biggest impact you might make in your new job is on the lives of those you manage. I didn't mean it would be a glorious job with all sorts of attaboys. No, it's largely a thankless job that doesn't depend directly on outside feedback. It's more self-motivated and is driven by your own innate sense of doing the right thing no matter how many others even see what you do.

Management is not easy, and very few people do it extremely well. A common thread in those who do, though, is this understanding of the difference between doing and managing. Look at it carefully and see how it creeps into every little part of your day, especially early on in the transition.

HANDLING PRESSURE

The fourth early discovery you'll make is that you didn't even know how to spell "p-r-e-s-s-u-r-e" before now! Yeah, you'll get a free pass this first time as you get up to speed, but then the honeymoon will be over and it's time to get to work, bud. It's not as if you didn't face pressure before your promotion, but the pressure was fairly predictable and it generally came from a very limited number of sources, like usually your boss.

Now, though, the pressure will come from many angles and you'll have to become adept at balancing all these competing demands from stakeholders (which is management speak for "people capable of sinking the ship if you don't keep them happy").

Adapting to this new kind of pressure will come amid the significant adjustment you're already making in transitioning from doing to managing, which we discussed above. So as you struggle with having more things to do but less time to do them, you'll feel like you're standing in the middle of a clearing while everybody else takes potshots at you. They'll be modern artists with paint guns and you'll be the unwitting canvas.

Pressure will come from the heightened expectation that you are ultimately responsible for things being done well. An inappropriate response would be to misunderstand that mandate and feel like you personally should be doing the work. You'll go nuts trying to do those things well, like we just saw in the previous section.

This might even be an easier pattern to slip into if your boss pressures you to do the work yourself. What you'll need to do is take that expression ("These things need to be done well, okay?") and translate it appropriately so that you help other people do these things well and not do them yourself.

Pressure will come from your new manager with his or her own agenda. Since pressure is typically delegated downward, you'll automatically inherent whatever pressure your supervisor feels.

Pressure will come from those you are managing, each with an individual agenda about their hours, their pay, their duties, their workspace, their benefits, their training, their clients, and on and on.

Pressure will come from your circle of influence outside work, each of whom will have freely shared ideas on how you should fulfill your role at work, how you should deal with the new boss, how to manage that problem employee, etc.

So, what's the best way to respond to all this pressure?

Start by determining what expectations really matter (like from your boss, to start), and what those expectations are. Get a written list of them, either directly from the boss (the ideal option), or just take notes yourself and send them back to your boss for approval. "This is what I heard you saying to me today. If I've misunderstood something, please let me know right away." There's just too much room for misinterpretation otherwise, by you and your boss.

It's unrealistic to have you to treat each expectation equally, and so the next step is to prioritize them. You can take a stab at it and pass them by your boss for approval, or you can ask your boss directly. I think you want to show as much initiative as possible with things like this. If your boss needs to correct you, you want him or her to rein you in, not prod you for more initiative.

Next, you'll have to reject the stupid expectations from your boss. In this category are the expectations that are likely redundant, without purpose, or just one of those "we've always done it this way" type of requests. By the way, I'm not suggesting that you call them stupid to people above you—just ignore them as appropriate. If you get some push back from upper management, ask them to help you re-prioritize. The best filter for stupid requests is money (fine, but it'll cost $x) or time (fine, but I'll not be able to work on x if I do that).

The next step is to begin filtering all of the management directives sent your way through the grid of these established expectations. Does this request fit? How? What will it displace? Do I have the resources and power to do it? Is it in conflict with another directive or the company's mission as a whole? You're not trying to get out of doing things or be difficult to work with. Instead, you're trying to be realistic and to "manage" things. And this would probably be the right place to talk about what that means. "Managing" something is not getting it done, necessarily, but handling it by anticipating (with plenty of advance notice) how it will be accomplished. If you operate under the assumption that managing is getting everything done, slowly you'll become an order-taker running next to the other rats on the treadmill.

Next, determine if you have both the authority and the resources to accomplish this task in the timeframe expected.

Let me make one final suggestion, here, and that's to always be honest in your progress reports to those above you on the food chain. Don't tell them what they want to hear, or what you think they want to hear. Tell them the truth.

HIRING THE RIGHT PEOPLE

The fifth early discovery you'll make is that there is a big difference between hiring people to help you do more and hiring people to take over the task and do things on their own, doing them even better than you would do them. It's seldom appropriate to hire young "blank slates" that can be filled with doing things the way they've always been done, and cheaply at that. No, you'll do better hiring experts who have something to teach you, right out of the gate. The bottom line—and one of the basic tenets espoused in this book—is this: hire people to help you do less, not to help you do more.

We're going to look at this in greater depth in a later chapter. But first, let's look at the different kinds of managers. You're just starting out on this path, and now's the time to get it right. You may be surprised to learn about this. Regardless, I think you'll find it heartening as you progress toward being a better manager.

6

The Different
Kinds of Managers

I began advising other business owners full-time in early 1994.
By that time, I'd also owned my own firm for six years and had
held various management positions before that. What I've
learned about management and the different kinds of managers
comes from all that experience, as well as the experience of being a parent. Since 1994, for example, I've had the privilege of
working with about fifty new business owners every year. With
that breadth of experience, it's pretty easy to make larger observations.

I've realized many things along this path, obviously, changing my mind in some key areas. In other words, I've been wrong.
One of those areas where I've been wrong is in my understand-

ing of the different kinds of managers. Let me start by telling you what I used to believe.

TWO KINDS OF MANAGERS

It seemed accurate and convenient, at first, to classify every manager as either a good one or a bad one. There didn't seem to be much mystery about it, either. Someone would ask me about my manager. I'd pause a few seconds, think about where the preponderance of the evidence seemed to point, and then pronounce that manager in question as being in one or the other of the two groups. "He's a good manager. I enjoy working there. Some things I don't agree with, but overall I'm glad to work for him." Or, "He's a bad manager. He's probably a good person, but he doesn't really know what he's doing when it comes to managing people. He never seems to be able to make a decision, and when he finally does get the courage to decide something, it's often too late and everyone on the sidelines wonders why it took him so long to acknowledge what everyone else knew was true a long time ago."

The more I'd make those observations about bad managers, though, the more I'd hear my own inconsistency. More specifically, it was obvious that my example of a bad manager, above, was really a description of a good person who wasn't managing. So their instincts were correct, but they refused to act on them, or acted with far too much delay.

Thus a change of mind occurred so that now I believe that there are three kinds of managers.

THREE KINDS OF MANAGERS

All the world of managers can be divided into three groups. The first group of managers is the one I'll just have to call evil people. One thing that leads me unmistakably to this conclusion is having surveyed and then interviewed every employee of hundreds of business owners. Employees aren't always right, and there are times when even the majority of employees are wrong, but when the employee consensus and my own observations agree, well, there's nothing left to do but state the obvious: we have an evil manager on our hands.

How many of them are there? I have no idea, but in my personal experience, I've encountered one in every fifty or so, or two percent.

These people regularly resort to humiliating people, stealing the credit for good work, lying about even the silliest things, and aligning people against each other behind their backs. I don't think there's anything that I as an outside consultant can do, either, except stand up to them. They aren't likely to change, and anything I say isn't likely to fall in the category of forcing change. So, I just tell it like it is, try to provide some advice to employees directly that'll keep them sane (like suggesting that they quit and move on), and so on.

This all assumes that they slip through my "evil" radar and I work for them in the first place. Many (most?) times I have no idea that they're evil until I've begun to read the surveys, and then confirm it with on-site interviews. By then it's too late to back out, though, so I proceed. But if I see any hint that they might be evil, I don't take the engagement in the first place.

The second group of managers is comprised essentially of good people who simply aren't managing. Sadly, I'd have to say that this represents the largest group of managers. They're not evil and they have good instincts, but they stop short of actually making decisions and then acting on them. We'll take a more in-depth look at this group in a moment.

The third group of managers, and the second largest, is comprised essentially of good people who are managing. They don't stand out because they get everything right but because they are active, both in their managing activity and in their presence. They know what they want, they observe what they're getting, and they make distinguishing decisions about the gaps between the two.

Put differently, they aren't remarkable managers because they always make the right decisions but because they act even before the fog lifts and the recommended action is obvious! That, my friend, is the essence of good management. Having a vision and forging ahead to make it happen even when the answers aren't obvious.

I like to call that making digital decisions in an analog world. Or, think of an animal crossing the road on a lonely, dark evening. Out of nowhere comes a truck, screaming straight toward them. The animal must decide to move to the right or the left, because staying right there is certain death. The direction chosen might very well mean death, too, but that's the price of taking the initiative.

WHAT PROMPTS GOOD PEOPLE TO NOT MANAGE

I've noticed some patterns by observing the people in that largest group: generally good people who aren't managing. They seem to take that approach for one (or a combination) of these reasons.

First, some people don't manage because they were promoted for the wrong reasons, as we've already seen. E.g., maybe they think they're to model the skill of the craft and not get dragged down to management issues. Or maybe they were promoted to continue the status quo without any overt leadership. Regardless, if their promotion was not ostensibly made in order to encourage their exercising of management, they may not feel the freedom (or need) to actually manage.

Second, some people don't manage because they don't have role models. I've never had an ideal, somewhat complete role model for management, and I don't know how important it is to have one. Or whether or not it's even possible. It seems more likely that we'll take parts and pieces of a certain management style a person exhibits and ignore their obvious failings. Doing that with several people will in the end yield something approaching a composite "ideal manager" that we can emulate.

Still, it's possible that someone may not have worked for enough people, hasn't worked for the right ones, or simply wasn't observant enough to take note of the areas in which managers provided good examples.

Third, some people don't manage because they care too much about being liked, and they think that there's a stronger likelihood of being liked if they don't act than if they make the wrong decision. That's nonsense, of course, but in the moment it feels true. "Surely these people can see how I'm agonizing over the right course of action and won't hold my lack of initiative against me. I'm just trying to do the right thing."

What they're really trying to do, though, is minimize the number of people unhappy with them, and that's not managing at all. At the heart of their delayed management is this belief that certainty must emerge from the fog of all the forces pulling on them to make certain decisions. That fog never lifts, though, and the very process of waiting for clarity hurts the culture and the management environment.

WHAT HAPPENS WHEN GOOD PEOPLE DON'T MANAGE

Many—maybe one-half—of the environments I've seen could be aptly described as managementless. That is, there's a good person in charge but that person isn't taking an active role in managing the operation. When I find that type of situation, the key is not to swap that person out for a better one, or even one with better instincts, but instead to encourage them to begin managing.

That invariably means getting them to act on their instincts, because after quizzing them about specific management situations it's very clear to me that they really do have the right instinct about what to do. They're just paralyzed about actually doing it.

What does an environment like that look like, you ask? I'm going to walk through the four results I've seen when good people aren't managing. Hopefully that will help you diagnose a situation where you could be managing more than you are, but it might also serve as a strong deterrent to inactivity on your part. See if you can recognize yourself or a former manager in any of these scenarios.

Loss of Respect. The thing about not managing is that nothing changes about the expectation that others have of you. Put differently, you can decide to not manage, but you cannot change the expectation that others have that you should be managing.

So, the longer you resist your management duties, the greater the loss of respect. This will impact other things, too, even when you're doing the right things. All of a sudden your opinions won't have the same impact. Even your example-setting activities will fall short because your failings as a manager will throw a shadow on everything you do.

Remember, though, that you aren't as likely to lose respect by doing the wrong things as a manager. No, you're more likely to lose respect by not doing anything.

That's an unforgivable sin: to see that something requires a manager's input and to sit idly by. It's so serious in the employee's mind that they lose respect for you.

Empowering of the Complaint-Sink. Do you know what a "heat sink" is on a circuit board? It's the portion that's built into the design to intentionally draw away damaging heat from the other components, where it can dissipate without harm. A "complaint sink" is my term for that person who gathers bad news, magnifies the complaints, and essentially gives them new life.

This is possible because of the passive management environment, which never lasts for long because something will fill that vacuum. People simply cannot be unmanaged, so in your absence as a manager, someone else will herd and then corral the flock. How they do that is with information, and nothing rises in a passive management like bad information about you. Negativity is gathered, nurtured, hoarded, and then spread at the most inopportune moments possible.

I don't know the person by name, but you know who I'm talking about!

Seeking Significance Via Relationship. All humans, in a work environment, seek significance. The safer means of finding that significance is to carve out a sandbox, or have someone do it for you, and then "do" things in that sandbox for which only you receive credit. Your area of influence is defined and the impact you have is measurable.

Absent such an arrangement, an employee is left to fend on their own to achieve significance, and they often resort to finding it via a strong relationship to the manager. When that occurs, it's no longer about what they do but who they know, and it becomes unhealthy.

This is a very common result in a passive management environment. The lack of role definition and resulting accountability yields employees who are scrambling for significance as they try to read the signals in an attempt to divine what the manager wants. We'll look at this in greater depth later.

Doing Everything...But the Work Itself. In an actively managed work environment, there are clearer boundaries in the work/life balance of both employees and managers. When they're at work, they work and they work hard. There's good structure, good processes, and good accountability. There are things to do and people to do them and clear boundaries along the path of getting them done.

In a passive management environment, though, there are all sorts of things to talk about, and most of those things get in the way of doing good work. Breaks are longer, people stand around chatting about how things could be different, and there's less motivation to do a great job. Even the teamwork isn't as strong.

Here's another way to look at that: your job as a manager is to clear all the obstacles from getting work done, to give them the tools to get work done, and then to protect them along the way.

You know what, though? Even though your management style is critical, it all starts with who you're managing. No matter how good a manager you are, you'll seldom turn bad employees into good ones, and so that's why we need to look at finding great employees next and then building on that.

7

Finding Those Who
Can Be Managed Well

No matter how good a manager you are, you'll have very little success turning bad employees into good ones. I've seen it done, but the odds are strongly against it. Even if you succeed at doing just that, though, the effort will be exhausting. So it's a much better idea to find the right people in the first place and then manage them well—a much better experience for all.

Having great employees begins with having the sort of environment where people want to work. Just like you might have a marketing plan to spread the word about your positioning and attract prospects to the client roster, so too might you have an internal marketing plan to spread the word about your culture so that you always have a large group of people anxious and eager to work for you. And if I were pressed to determine which of those "marketing" efforts was more important to the firm, I'd usually say it's the latter: give me good employees who are managed well and together we'll figure out the rest. Good clients just aren't enough, frankly.

So this starts with your culture, which we'll discuss in depth in a later chapter. Assuming you have a culture where people want to work, though, how would you go about spreading the word about that culture?

Thankfully, your primary means of spreading the word are the employees themselves. How many times have you been visiting a friend only to have the conversation quickly move to employment: "How are things going at your job?" Boom. In that second, you have an advocate or not. An advocate will say, "Great! I really love my job. I feel like I am challenged, I have an impact, and I really like the people I work with."

This gets filed away in the prospective employee's mind and when that person is looking for work—now or later—they'll be drawn to any opportunity that seems to be a fit. Because of the culture.

SPREADING THE CULTURE

You want to spread the word about your great culture, far and wide. Here are some ideas that might help.

Vendors. Appreciative vendors should always be included in searches for prospective employees. Not only will they have an insider's knowledge of your field, but they will have worked with multiple candidates and will have worked with many of them individually.

All this presupposes, of course, that your vendors are appreciative and want you to succeed. If you constantly beat them up over price or expect them to perform the heroic day after day, forget about including them on your cheerleading squad.

Clients. Not only will clients know of candidates who might want to work for you, they love hearing that you're growing, changing, and adapting. Let them refer candidates, even from the client side (if appropriate for that position). In fact, some of your best employees will come from the client side.

The other advantage of using contented clients as advocates for prospective employees is that they like to have a say in who they are working with. So in hiring someone they've recommended, you can easily cement an even stronger relationship between your firm and the client.

Employees. Employees, obviously, understand the culture better than anyone, so who better to find prospective employees who would be a good match.

The organizational development people tell us that one key to keeping great employees is to provide an environment where one of their best friends is someone they work with. So, bringing a known friend into the field not only ensures fewer surprises but encourages longevity in the workplace.

Awards. Even though the judging process is a little arbitrary, it can't hurt to win an award for being a "Top Place to Work." Word about that spreads, too, and you'll end up with a larger pool of candidates from which to choose.

They don't all have to be those types of awards, either. Nearly as effective are any industry-specific awards. It provides publicity for your firm, but more than that it provides the right kind of publicity.

Gallery Showings. Is your culture one of exploration and curiosity? Do you like to hire balanced, cultured, and intelligent employees? If so, consider building an art gallery into your facility, and then feature local artists and photographers for a rotating exhibit. Each showing (which changes every two months) might kick off with an open house and a tour of the rest of the office. You'll find that just the right kind of prospective employee will attend. Plus, you'll get a chance to mingle in a more relaxed setting.

Educational Referrals. Develop a relationship with any schools (undergraduate and graduate) that award degrees typical of the ones held by your employees. Offer to speak to a class or two every semester, and then ask the professors to be on the lookout for that occasional outstanding student that might need an internship and/or job placement. You probably only want the top one or two students, but over time they can make a terrific addition to your firm, particularly if they've had a chance to work for you under a paid internship arrangement first.

Industry Gatherings. What clubs or associations do your prospective employees frequent and/or belong to? Is there a vehicle that accepts advertising or job postings? Having seen the inside of many of these, nearly all of them have struck me as being primarily about networking...not for the good of the businesses they represent but in order to move up to a better position. So, this type of purpose is clearly on their minds and it's worth taking advantage of that.

Self-Promotion/Branding. Most of your own branding and self-promotion is undertaken specifically to find clients, but there are secondary purposes, too. For example, employees often tell me that they feel proud to work for a company that promotes itself, especially if it's done well.

Another benefit of self-promotion is that it gets prospective employees to take notice and think well of your firm, making it more likely that they'll think of you when a position opens.

Your Website. Your website is not just a place where prospective clients evaluate your firm and gauge their own level of interest in working for you. Employees of other firms spend many hours surfing the websites of their employer's competitors, and if you're on that list, you might as well be catering a portion of the website's message to them.

How? Well, for starters it's a good idea to have very personable photos of employees who are obviously content and glad to be working there. It also makes sense to give them a hand in describing the culture, capturing moments of their everyday work life in an interesting fashion. You might ask them to shoot videos of unstaged, roving interviews of their coworkers, even.

One firm I know has taken this to an entirely different level. The principal hosts a webinar every three months for prospective employees. They get to hear first hand about upcoming opportunities and participate in a question and answer session with the principal. Where else could they get a better feel for the firm than that?

Annual Events. Consider an annual event, perhaps at a sports venue or club. All your employees would attend, and you'd invite the industry for several hours of relaxed fun. They'll get to rub shoulders with each other in a setting more conducive to "talking about how work is going for you."

Co-Placement with HR Departments. If your firm is located in a secondary or tertiary geographic market, contact the HR department of the large employers nearby and make sure they know about your job openings. Often they'll be tasked with not only finding a job for the key employee they'd like to bring aboard, but also for that key employee's spouse (who will be moving with them).

Everybody wins in this arrangement: both employees and both companies. And the partnership might very well lead to other benefits after you begin working together.

Social Media. As long as it doesn't become a bottomless pit of time, it can make sense to establish and then nurture a presence in social media, particularly if the effort is led by someone of the appropriate age group who is also savvy about the medium. There should be sporadic contributions by the principal, but it would not be a good use of the principal's time to go beyond that.

Direct Contact. If there's someone you really want to work for you, chances are that they are employed at a competitor. Why not just pick up the phone and call them? You might or might not call them at work, but there's no reason not to call them. If that person is very happy where they are and the environment is a good one, your call is not a threat because they'll stay.

You poach clients all the time—I'm not sure why it should be any different for employees.

Advertising. And then, of course, there's always the more overt advertising you might place when trying to fill a specific position.

All of this is designed to get you plenty of the right candidates from which to choose. If you start with the right people, managing them well is so much easier.

So you have this group of very qualified candidates. How do you screen them so that the best candidates rise to the top? That's what we'll look at next.

8

Screening Good Candidates

If picking out the right shoes is more relevant to your comfort than how you wear them, choosing the right employees is certainly the better part of good management practice. An extra hour or two of thoughtful consideration will save you countless hours of management hassle. Never mind the tens of thousands of dollars in lost opportunity, grudging severance allotments, and finding the dear departed one's replacement.

Obviously, something is wrong with the typical selection process. If job candidates are to be believed, nearly every one of them is interested, enthusiastic, and eager. They have vast experience, they display a willingness and ability to learn new skills, and money isn't the deciding factor.

Right. Somebody certainly isn't telling the truth, and it's your job to root out the imposters.

EVEN BEFORE THE INTERVIEW

This process of screening applicants begins with the résumé (see specifics below). From there you move to some basic reference checking to verify employment data. Next it would be common practice to send the candidate a clear job description with attendant expectations for the job, along with a request that they provide salary history (not salary requirements, which are less relevant). Assuming you haven't seen any red lights yet, continue with a phone interview. Not only will this be a good test of their phone skills, but you can make a decision to eliminate—or continue to pursue—a candidate with a ten-minute investment.

In this process it wouldn't be uncommon to grant phone interviews to twenty percent of the applicants, and then to grant personal interviews to twenty percent of those who were interviewed by phone.

You can easily delegate the administrative part of this, but you don't dare delegate so much of it that you lose sufficient opportunities to interact with the applicant. It's difficult to imagine something in your day that's more important than this.

WHAT TO WATCH FOR IN THE RÉSUMÉ

There are specific things to watch for as you review a résumé. The first, and perhaps most obvious, would be typos, coupled with grammatical errors. Frankly, perfect grammar and spelling isn't critical to a production type role, but if the person is involved in customer service, new business development, or management, credibility will be hard to come by unless written communication skills are adequate.

Look for gaps in employment. They might indicate a legitimate break from employment to take care of an ailing relative, or they might indicate that someone was fired and/or they were largely unemployable. You have a legitimate interest in this.

As you wade through the résumé, circle any vague performance claims such as "grew company's bottom line net by 13 percent." At first glance that seems specific, but it's meaningless without the full context.

Look too at training accomplishments that seem to be inflated. Did the applicant attend a $99 seminar, or was it a recognized continuing education experience?

Make sure you can make sense of the person's titles. In particular, try to separate management over projects from management over people. The rule of thumb is this: they didn't manage people unless they gave them performance reviews and at least made recommendations on their salary.

Scan the references and see how direct they are. In other words, do they list former supervisors at recent jobs, or are they associates, professors, or friends of the family. The latter would usually not be of much use.

Finally, note the average tenure at a company. It's not so important if they changed jobs within the company, but moving quickly from company to company is usually not good. It points to easily being dissatisfied, quitting when things get tough, or not exercising good judgment when accepting new positions.

SAFETY IN NUMBERS

Have several people meet with the applicant individually. There is so much at stake that several opinions are safer than just yours (or whoever is doing the hiring). To ensure that the feedback you get is independent, capture the interviewer's perspective before they compare it with your perspective, or the perspective of others who have interviewed the applicant.

The best way to ensure objectivity in this regard is to ask that the interviewer record their impressions in writing before emerging from the interview setting. If it's offsite, ask them to go home and compose an email with their thoughts. First impressions are very critical, and unless you capture them before group comparison, the collective opinion of the candidate will resemble the opinion of the most communicative in your employee group.

What about group interviews? It's best to use them sparingly. Not only are they intimidating to the prospective employee, but they usually result in an artificially uniform opinion of the job candidate.

If you decide to use group interviews to screen applicants, make sure the "victim" knows in advance so they can get their will in order. You might also ensure that it's a rounded or oval seating arrangement to avoid a "trial" setting. The interviewing group can also meet in advance and agree roughly on who is going to ask which question, at the same time pledging not to interrupt or argue with each other!

Finally, consider asking at least one outside person to meet briefly with the candidate. This could be your management consultant, a key client, your accountant, an important vendor, or your personal coach. The particular position being filled will dictate the most appropriate party to meet them.

WHAT TO WATCH FOR IN THE INTERVIEW

Other than the specific words that they utter, there are several things to watch for in an interview. First, determine something about their personality type. There are many sources for this information, and you'll readily find them with a search. Being conscious of how they interact with their environment will help you interview them better. It will also help you determine how well they will work with people in their department. At some point you might even have a third party conduct an actual interview.

Early on, make sure you shake their hand. If you are seated at a desk when they are ushered in, walk out from behind it. Always step forward with your arm outstretched as a sign of respect and warmth. Wielding intimidation and power is short sighted, and even your nervousness can be misinterpreted as the same thing. Obviously, see how they react, too. Are they passive, aggressive, or somewhere in between? How firm is their handshake?

Specifically note how they are dressed. You can expect the applicant with little prior knowledge to dress a little better than they normally would. Are they formal, garish, relaxed, sloppy? Every piece helps complete the puzzle.

Note where and how they sit. You might direct them to a specific chair, but they might inch it toward or away from you. Even if they don't move it, they'll certainly sit back, upright, or forward. What does that tell you about this person and how they'll typically interact?

How appropriate is the length of their answers? At first, they will likely be too short or too long, simply because they are nervous. But once they become comfortable, try to judge their conversational aptitude. Some people tend to be abrupt and uncommunicative. Others are boring and ponderous and repetitive. Note your instincts, taking your own personality into account (e.g., you may be less patient than the average person they'll work with).

WHAT NOT TO WATCH FOR IN THE INTERVIEW

Having pointed out the things you should watch for, allow me to mention a few things you shouldn't be too picky about. Don't look for someone like you. Your firm will benefit more from someone not like you (no offense). The last thing we need is a firm full of clones. So if you are the no nonsense analytical type hiring a sales person, don't be offended by their exuberance! Everybody's not like you.

Second, don't worry if the person isn't totally comfortable, even by the end of the interview. Some very valuable people with tremendously useful skills will never interview well. That fact should count against them if they manage people or have significant client contact, but otherwise keep going without discounting them too early.

WHERE TO CONDUCT THE INTERVIEW

Interviews should be conducted in the most appropriate places. You might have to compromise if the interview is being held at an airport or if your office space isn't all that private, but whenever possible look for an interview location with specific attributes.

The interview location should be organized no matter where it is, but particularly if it is in your office. The interviewee should have a comfortable chair so that they are not distracted during the conversation. The area should be well ventilated, too, which means plenty of air that is not too hot or too cold. Be sensitive about open windows behind you that might blind your visitor.

The room should be private as well as quiet. This means that the door should be closed, your phone should not accept calls, and people should be instructed to not interrupt you.

Be as close to the prospect as you can (like each of you on one side of a small table), but not so close that they can read any notes you make.

Have water available for each of you. Stay away from food or snacks. In fact, don't conduct an interview in a restaurant. It's not quiet or private, and you won't be able to cut it off early.

PREPARING FOR THE INTERVIEW

To make the best use of your time in the interview, gather all the information you'll need. At a minimum this should include their résumé, any material necessary for a general orientation to the company (employee handbook, etc.), and copies of the marketing materials you might be using to position the firm. Note your questions about the résumé on the résumé itself.

Write out some simple questions to start with, and leave the more difficult ones for later (see below).

Be sure you know the job responsibilities and the qualifications/skills required for that job. Think a bit about the personality and temperament that would be ideal for the job before you meet the candidate, not after.

CONDUCTING THE INTERVIEW

Start off with something easy and comfortable. That usually means a tour so that they begin to get comfortable with you, meet the gang, and absorb the spirit of your firm through the décor and organization (now that's a terrifying thought, eh?).

When you are finished with the tour, offer to get them a beverage. Always take the lead and keep them informed of what's coming next.

Don't be driven by an agenda, but do make it evident that you have one. When you walk through how things are going to unfold, explain how long you think everything will take. That will be the time to discover if they need to leave at a certain time. It also helps with pacing so that you leave enough time for questions.

As soon as you sit down, give them an accurate picture of the job. A formal description will help, but even a verbal one is useful. If appropriate, include the career path that leads to and from this job. This is also the perfect time to talk about salary range lest you end up overpaying someone simply because of longevity. Once they have hit that salary range, they can only expect to make more than cost of living increases if the company becomes significantly larger (with an increase in responsibility for that position), or the employee moves to a higher paid position.

Start with easy questions to get them comfortable. Then move to the questions that require greater reflection and articulation.

Finally, give them a chance to ask any questions they might have before closing the interview.

Here's one warning that you might keep in mind: don't hint at things in the interview unless you fully intend to make them happen. Usually the offending remarks relate to "a new retirement plan," "an ownership sharing plan," or some other employee benefit. It's best not to mention anything that isn't already in place or specifically in progress.

IMPORTANCE OF THE RIGHT INTERVIEW QUESTIONS

The right questions are not too scripted. Ask the same questions everyone else does and the prospective employee will not feel valued. Worse yet, you'll get the answers they've already formulated in anticipation of the stock questions! So forget asking them which supervisors were the most difficult, what they liked least about their previous job, what work related problem they faced recently, and the details about the best decision they ever made.

Make them your own. Be yourself. But whatever you ask, don't include discriminatory questions. This renders several topics off limits, like national origin, citizenship, maiden name, religion, marital status, parental status, personal activities, age, or financial status. Even though these topics are all off limits, there are plenty of other good ones. Your goal should be to be remembered as fair, interesting, and intelligent.

Even reading through a résumé, there are many things you don't know yet, like their actual responsibilities, how they approach their work, and what objectives they are seeking in a new employment situation. You'll also want to explore their short and long term goals, their compatibility with other department members, and their actual skill level. Your questions should be designed to surface this information and more.

GOOD QUESTIONS TO ASK

Here are some questions you might ask once you are past the easy, comfortable ones. These are a little different from the norm, which means that you aren't likely to encounter canned responses. In parentheses you'll find something of what the answers will tell you.

It would be helpful if you could describe a significant failure or two that you've been part of and directly responsible for, as well as how that's made you smarter. (Do they admit failure? Are they honest and realistic?)

Though you don't need to name specific companies, tell me how many other jobs you are seriously considering, and something about them: size, focus, position, etc. (Do they really know what they want, or are they just fishing everywhere?)

What makes you stand out among your peers? (Can they be confident without being arrogant?)

How do you handle situations where direct reports are performing unacceptably? (What is their management style like?).

Based on your limited first impressions, tell me what strikes you as good and bad about how this company has treated you to date. (How observant and forthright are they?)

In what situations would you have the least amount of patience at work? (What are the pressure points we'll face?)

What role does work have in your personal life, and how do you balance the different elements? (How hard will they work? How burnt out might they be? How distracting will their personal life be?)

How much structure, direction, and feedback is part of your ideal work environment? How much do you like to provide to those who might work for you? (Will they be a control freak, too hands-off, or closed to feedback?)

If you don't get a new job, how will you work/interact differently where you are now? (How willing are they to adapt to tough situations rather than just giving up?)

If your boss would give me a truthful answer, what would they love and hate about your work? (Are they self-aware enough to know how they impact others?)

What do you hear about this company in the community? (Have they done their homework?)

Relate to me a time when your personal standards/ethics would not allow you to comply with what a supervisor was asking. How did you handle it? (How do they handle conflict? How principled are they? Do they magnify disagreement where issues could have been smoothed over?)

Based on what you've learned so far, what are you most excited about in relation to this opportunity? What are you most concerned about? (How should you structure the offer to them? What can you clarify?)

DIGGING DEEPER

As you work through your own questions or the ones above, there will be times when the prospective employee doesn't elaborate as much as you'd like. For just those times you'll want a few tools to steer the conversation deeper.

The first thing to try is to repeat or restate the question. That will establish that they have not answered it. If they've answered part of it, rephrase it to narrow down your particular interest.

You can also ask them to give you another example, or extend the discussion by saying: "what did that teach you about [blank]?"

If all else fails, just sit silently. Awkwardness can be a good thing, particularly if the other person buckles first! They'll frequently feel obligated to fill the silence.

WHAT YOU ARE LOOKING FOR

Obviously, you are looking for information not otherwise at hand in the résumé or easily verified from references. But in a less tangible sense, you are trying to gauge whether or not this candidate is honest, deferential, open, confident, and comfortable having a point of view.

On the other hand, you are hoping that you don't find undue nervousness, evasiveness, or arrogance.

ENDING THE INTERVIEW

As the interview begins to wind down (and you should keep it on schedule unless you have sought and received their permission to extend it), tell them what you'll do now, how you'll contact them next, and roughly when this will happen. Ask them for any other information you feel is missing and find out when you might receive it.

With the appropriate permission, give them a list of either the direct phone extensions or home phone numbers of employees. Encourage them to call any of them and ask any question they'd like. Nothing communicates an open work environment more than this, because it helps them see that there won't be any surprises when they come to work with you.

Ask them to call if something changes. This might include a different timetable for their switching jobs, another job offer, a change in their spouse's employment, or anything else that would help you construct an appropriate job offer.

If you are conducting several interviews back to back, leave sufficient time between them. Not only will this make it easier in case you run long, but it will also enable you to catch up on note taking while your impressions are fresh and unsoiled by your contact with the next applicant.

Finally, consider doing some testing if you still have questions or the particular job requires specific, measurable skills. This might include sales aptitude screening, writing skills, personality profiling, a creative assignment, or exercises in particular software packages.

AFTER THEY LEAVE

Quickly write down your impressions before talking with others about them. They need to be your impressions, not your impressions mingled with the impressions of others.

Next, slip out of your office and ask the front desk person what they thought of this individual. Better yet, ask them ahead of time to be observant so that they'll have something to say when you ask that question later. How did they wait, what did they read, how did they treat the front desk person?

And soon after they leave, send the applicant a "homework" request via email, with a time frame, to test their writing ability and their promptness. It could be something like this: "Julie, it was nice to meet you today. After you left I was thinking about one of your responses, and it led to another question in my mind. Can you take a stab at penning just a few paragraphs in response to this question [list it]? If it's possible, please get back to me by [date]. Thanks."

FINALLY

So let's skip ahead and assume that you've narrowed all these good candidates down to your top choice, made an offer, and now they'll join you on a specific date.

Now it's time to prepare a warm welcome in the form of an excellent orientation program, which we'll look at next.

9
Integrating Employees Well

The impetus for including this chapter came from sitting down and talking with thousands of employees since 1994. A common refrain was how poorly these new employees were integrated into their respective firms. They seldom shared this with any resentment, but it was clear that their early experience could have been so much better if the orientation itself had been more comprehensive.

OUR DILEMMA

I have not measured this scientifically, but in working with hundreds of firms I would guess that maybe twenty percent have a formal orientation checklist for new employee integration. Of that twenty percent, perhaps one-half use the list. In other words, employees are being integrated on an ad hoc basis, and the process is being reinvented each time. There are probably three reasons for this.

First, there is no group efficiency in regularly scheduled, large group orientation. So many employees move in and out of large companies that they can hold an orientation every Monday, for example, and that's when you start. In your case, only one employee is starting at a time, typically.

Second, your firm may be too small to have a dedicated Human Resources (HR) department, and so whoever is responsible for doing the orientation is also in charge of many other things. The potential for distraction is very real.

Third, you decide to hire the new employee because you are busy, which means that you have the least amount of time to spend on a careful orientation. Stated differently, you have the least amount of time when the new employee needs it most.

Add the pressure that you feel for them to produce quickly—and the pressure they feel on their own to produce quickly—and you have a recipe that yields sloppy orientation. Instead of boot camp, you are grabbing someone off the street and dropping them from an airplane behind enemy lines. It's sink or swim.

THE IMPORTANCE OF ORIENTATION

To motivate you to implement this at your firm, let me list six reasons why a strong orientation is critical. You've likely gotten by without much planning, but the return on this investment is substantial.

First, you'll eliminate this major "memory maker" for new employees. Inadequate orientation sticks with the employee for years, so why not give them a positive starting point? I've heard many employees say: "I love my job, but it was a really rough start."

Second, you'll realize significant gains in productivity. In fact, you'll gain far more in productivity than you'll lose in time spent developing and implementing the orientation program.

Third, your firm will gain a good reputation among the prospective employee pool. Freshly integrated recruits will spread the word among friends who work elsewhere, and they will also mention their positive experience when they interact with job candidates.

Fourth, a positive orientation experience will result in less employee turnover. A study by Rebecca Ganzelin in 1998 demonstrated that a structured orientation made it sixty percent more likely that an employee would be productive for at least three years. Better yet, those same employees reached full productivity two months earlier than those who did not work through a structured orientation.

Two years later Pope Ward discovered that one-half of employees move on within three years, largely because they are not exposed to experienced veterans, they have difficulty acclimating to the culture, they receive limited early training, and the expectations that others have of them are not made clear.

Fifth, a complete orientation can eliminate irritation and tension for you. This occurs when the new employee violates an unwritten rule and stumbles into a transgression without any warning. Do you have a specific way you want the phone answered? Tell him. Do you always want a fax cover sheet used when sending something to a client? Tell her.

Sixth, new employees experience more "job remorse" in the absence of orientation. The trial by fire they experience reinforces any of the normal misgivings they might have about a job, whereas a complete orientation will quell them. Taking a new job is almost always a compromise, and integrating them effectively can only heighten their experience and lessen their doubts.

A CHECKLIST

What follows are dozens of suggestions from which you'll want to pick and choose to tailor your own program. The list is designed to be comprehensive, and you'll want nearly all the items on your list. Most can be handled in less than a minute. A few will take more than an hour.

These suggestions are divided into six groups. Each group of items should be handled by a different person. Not only will each person know the most about a given subject, but the new employee will be able to bond with their particular contact for that section. (Long term, unless the new employee is working with one of their best friends, they will not stay on at your firm, as I mentioned above.) Here are the suggestions, after which I'll provide some ideas on how to implement an orientation program.

ADMINISTRATIVE ASSISTANT OR RECEPTIONIST

Tour and Introductions. Have the responsible party first walk them through the entire facility to meet everybody and to get the layout of the office.

Office Gift. Though this is not properly a checklist item, have the leader of this section put together a welcome package of assorted items, which can then be placed at the person's new workspace. It might include office supplies, candy, bottled drinks, a lunch certificate, and "stupid question" coupons, which they can hand to anyone without fear of ridicule!

Home Gift. This same person should have a gift delivered to the new employee's home, to be there when they get home after their first day. It sends a nice signal to any significant other living with them, and it sets the tone for the beginning of the orientation.

Workspace. This should be all ready for the employee when they arrive, not later, and not even soon after. First, have business cards printed, checking with the new employee about how they want their name to be listed, and checking with the supervisor about a title, if any, with a supply mailed to their home. It'll engender pride and let them hand the cards out as they tell others about their new job. Second, have a comfortable chair at their workstation. Third, have keys made, and ask the new employee to sign a statement acknowledging their receipt. Fourth, gather whatever information is necessary to update your firm's marketing materials (e.g., the bio pages you include with proposals or the staff listing on your website).

Parking. Explain where they should park, talk through parking lot safety, and discuss the firm's policy in parking reimbursement, if applicable. Be sure to point out any spots that are "reserved" for any important employees or clients, since there's nothing quite like parking in the boss' spot the first day without even knowing it.

Climate Control. Explain who is allowed to adjust the thermostat, and where it is. If it is on a timer, illustrate how to override the night settings if they work late or come in early.

Meetings. Detail the place for internal meetings (with employees) or meetings with clients, including where/when to reserve the room. Walk through the usual practice of getting a beverage for a client.

Local Food Resources. Hand the new employee a printed list of local eateries, including name, address, phone, type of food, and hours. If applicable, point out where you keep a copy of the menus. (This is the same list you would give to a client whose visit extends over the lunch period.)

Bulletin Boards. Point out the bulletin board and let the new employee know what material is posted there, so they'll watch for it, as well as what materials might be appropriate to post on their own.

Supplies. After showing them where the supplies are kept, explain how special orders are made. This is a good time to describe a recycling program.

Office Library. Note what publications you subscribe to, where back issues are kept, and the normal routing of these publications when they are received. Also note any policies associated with the books in your library.

Emergencies. Employees will need to know what they can expect in the event of inclement weather, as well as the procedures to react properly to a tornado, flood, fire, etc.

INFORMATION SYSTEMS

Computer. Have the IS manager, or whoever manages that function—even if they don't do it officially—walk the new employee through the use of their computer. This would include the process for storing files, printing, backup, installing software, etc.

Email Account. Set up the new employee's email address, being sure to check with them about their preferred address (as long as it fits within established conventions at your firm).

Codes. Provide the appropriate security codes for their computer, for the phone system, the office entrance, timekeeping, the copy machine, the fax machine, and the postage meter. Note where they should and should not be kept for privacy reasons.

Remote Work. Explain how the employee can check their email remotely, how they can log into the company web site to review work, and how they can keep their timekeeping records current even when they are not in the office.

Mobile Phone. If the employee is filling a position that requires the use of a cellular phone, set them up with the phone, manuals, charger, etc.

Listing on Web Site. If employees are listed on your web site, the IS manager should get an appropriate photo and data in order to update their listing immediately.

Phone System. The employee should be assigned a phone extension and given directions on how to get their voicemails (in and out of the office). But that's not all, given how important phone etiquette is in a service business. The new employee should be instructed on when to answer the phone (after so many rings) and what to say when they answer the phone, particularly if they are in a position that provides backup to the receptionist. Finally, they should receive direction on what to say in their voicemail greeting in different circumstances (traveling, vacation, etc.).

Conference Room Equipment. Many conference rooms are equipped with expensive equipment that also might be complicated. In order to create the right impression with clients, the new employee needs to know how to make a conference call or project a presentation through the projector. They might even want to be able to help a client hook up their own laptop when working in the conference room for an extended period.

IS Help. Finally, the new employee needs to know when to call for IS help, how the request should be routed, and how quickly they can expect the request to be handled.

PRINCIPAL

Initial Comments. Start by separating the business from yourself. In doing so, you'll invite a relationship that encourages free exchange. Otherwise, the new employee will find candor difficult, especially at the beginning of their tenure, always wondering if you'll take constructive criticism personally.

So in the middle of your statements about what your firm does well, talk about what you don't do well.

History. Share the history of your firm from your perspective. It will help them see why things are the way they are, and it will help them "buy" into where you are headed. In the end they might not agree with some of your policies, but at least they won't think you came about them in a vacuum.

Direction. Explain where your firm is headed. Talk about the size of your firm, the mix of services you offer, and where the larger industry is headed. Discuss your mission and philosophy for the company, whether it's written down or not.

Marketing. If your new hire is involved in new business development, there are few things more critical than getting specific direction from you on what clients to hunt for. But even if the new person is not involved in new business development, they will always have some impact on it, and it's good to give them some background. Do that by handing them the same materials a prospect might receive, a clear statement of your unique positioning in the marketplace, an elevator speech that expands on that positioning, and your policy on referrals.

Culture. Finally, let someone else write a humorous treatment of your firm's culture. Any copywriter on staff would gladly rise to the challenge, and the result will be a lighthearted piece without the pretension that might accompany an official document. We'll dive into this culture question in greater depth later.

SUPERVISOR

Pre-Announcement. Make sure existing employees are apprised of your progress in hiring, as long as it would be appropriate to do so. But no matter what the circumstances, make sure that the new employee's arrival does not serve as the announcement. It's not courteous to the new employee or their new coworkers.

Press Release. If you customarily issue a news release when a new hire is made, gather the necessary data so that it can be done in a timely manner. Some of this can be gleaned from their résumé and interview, but you might need to fill some holes before a news release can be crafted.

Client Visit. Arrange to take the new employee on a client visit. Inform the client that you'll be bringing them, just to eliminate any element of surprise. The new employee needs to experience how clients need to be treated, how familiar to be with them (eventually), how to show up on time, and how to debrief the client and staff properly. These things are important to learn no matter what their position since it puts their duties into context.

Role Definition. Make sure the new employee knows their role. Their title would be part of this, and might provide some indication of their duties, but a job description would be even more specific. Make sure the new employee knows who their single supervisor is. Yes, there should be a specific person, and it should be one person, not multiple supervisors.

Performance Goals. Are there specific performance expectations that are measurable? Be sure to surface them and put them in writing.

Introductory Period. If there is an introductory period, explain how long it is, as well as the basis upon which a decision will be made at the end. It's important to align expectations in this regard.

Dress Code. Don't assume the new employee will pick up the dress code by observation. It need not be strict, but the broad parameters should be delineated. Don't forget to distinguish between dress in the office and dress while on client visits.

Performance Reviews. Explain what will happen in the yearly salary review and monthly performance discussion. More on the monthly performance discussion in a later chapter.

Clerical Support. Every firm is different in terms of the clerical support they offer employees, and how to ask for it. Help them sidestep any land mines by being clear on these two points.

Client Communication. Detail the standards you expect for client communication by addressing how they should interact with clients via email, phone calls, letters, and faxes. Discuss tone, spelling errors, promptness, and anything else that is important to you.

Early Perspectives. As the new employee's supervisor, give them a small notebook and ask them to take the time to record as many first impressions they can think of, especially in their first two weeks. Encourage them to not filter any thought that comes to mind. Then, in two months, ask them to go back through their initial thoughts and share the ones they are comfortable disclosing to you. Both of these parts are essential, since first impressions can only be captured early on, but are best shared later when they are comfortable in their working relationships and not afraid to be candid.

PROJECT MANAGEMENT

Workflow. Walk the employee through the life of a typical job. How does it start? What paperwork is required? Who needs to be kept in the loop? Will the employee be involved in estimating? How much time is allotted for tasks?

Files. Where are files kept, and is it customary for the employee to keep them at his/her desk while the project is in process? What is kept in the file and what is discarded?

Regular Meetings. Explain any regular project management meetings that are held (e.g., the first Monday), and whether the employee is expected to attend them.

Purchase Orders. Note whether or not the employee can authorize outside purchases, and whether a purchase order must be utilized to do so.

Timesheets. Most importantly in this section, explain that the purpose of timesheets is to improve future estimating, not measure performance. Be specific about how often they are to be kept (every fifteen minutes), when they are to be turned in (every day, before they leave), and how to use the codes in use at your firm.

HUMAN RESOURCES

Requisite Paperwork. Handle any required paperwork, preferably later in the day. This would include payroll withholding forms, proof of their right to work, insurance (health, disability, dental, and life), and the receipt for the delivery of their handbook. In the same category, mention the retirement options they'll be eligible for later, explain their employee classification (exempt or non-exempt), note how reimbursements are handled, and provide a blank copy of your firm's performance evaluation form.

Exclusivity. Walk through your policy on freelancing, and have them sign copies of your "non-compete" agreement and your non-disclosure agreement. These should have been given to them during the interviewing process, and if they do not sign them the first day, they should not be allowed to return until they do.

Training. If there is a policy whereby employee training costs are reimbursed, explain that to the new employee.

Music. Make sure the new employee understands the policy on music in the workplace. This is a frequent source of tension with new employees.

Work Hours. Clarify when employees are expected to arrive for work, what arrangements are typical for lunch, when employees normally leave work for the day, how vacations are scheduled, what holidays are observed, what smoking breaks are allowed, and whether or not there is a recurring employee retreat, especially if it involves non-standard hours, such as a Saturday morning.

Client Orientation. One of the final things the new employee should do is to sit down with "orientation files" on each of the major clients. This would include a list of key personnel, samples of what you've done, key trends, etc.

Company Resources. Let employees know the acceptable parameters for using company equipment, software, and office supplies.

There are two other critical parts to this: internet access and personal calls, whether they involve long distance charges or not.

IMPLEMENTATION

Seem like a lot of work? Not really, since you already have the checklist. Here are some ways to smooth the way.

Checklist. Go through the suggestions above and do your own checklist. Actually make it a checklist, too, so that a quick skim will indicate whether each item has been covered.

It's also better to have one checklist that is used for everyone. Just mark through the items that might not apply to a particular new employee.

Handbook. You are going to need a handbook, too. If you don't already have one, the list above might be a good starting place. Your handbook should cover much more than an orientation checklist, and in some cases that list can just refer the new employee to the appropriate place in your handbook. But a handbook is more about policies, and an orientation checklist is more about integration.

Divided Responsibilities. Take your list and divide it by subject. Then assign each section to the appropriate person. Make sure the appropriate person is prepared and mentally ready to take some time from their schedule to help. And hopefully they'll be in a good mood on orientation day!

One Full Day. Orientation should generally occur over one full day. It's better to allot as much time as might be necessary so that nothing is rushed.

Buddy for One Week. In addition to the individuals who will guide the new employee through each stage of the orientation, a new employee should be assigned a "buddy" who will check in on them frequently during the first week. The new employee will also be able to go to this person first with questions that might seem silly.

Meeting at One Week Anniversary. When the new employee starts, a meeting should be scheduled one week from that start date. This meeting should be set and managed by their immediate supervisor. It will be an opportunity for the employee to ask any questions that are more appropriate for management, and it will allow the manager to correct any initial performance issues. It's difficult to have too much communication, especially early in the new employee's career.

Expectations. You'll measure new employees against your own expectations for them, whether you are forthright about them or not. What do you expect of the new employee? How soon do you expect them to be up to speed? There's no magic answer, but if you've hired the right person, the answer should probably be within one to three months. And the right person is defined as someone who has something to teach your firm, not someone who needs training.

Recruitment. Don't forget to use this checklist in the recruitment and interviewing stages. It will definitely set your firm apart as they consider their options. The message they'll receive is that you are organized, thoughtful, and respectful.

Hopefully this will help you integrate employees well with a specific orientation procedure. They'll appreciate it, and so will you. Next we want to look more specifically at structuring roles.

10

Structuring Roles

Of the many things you work through as a manager, determining how to structure roles—especially yours—seems to be a perennial struggle. This chapter will give you some big picture thoughts so that you can take it further on your own, with more specificity.

MEANING OF GROWTH

As you may have already realized, most structural problems occur by letting growth happen to you. And you let it happen to you because you might misunderstand what it means. Here are three quick points to make about growth.

First, it does not necessarily mean that you'll make more money if you are a firm or department with more employees.

In some cases, there is actually an inverse relationship between size and net profit. Statistically, the percentage of net profit often drops as the firm adds employees. The actual net profit is larger, but not "per employee." So, disabuse yourself of the notion that you have to be large to make money.

Second, growing does not always mean that you'll be able to snag larger client relationships. There is some truth to this, but it's not absolute. You can still play on a pretty big stage even as a smaller firm.

Third, what growth always means is that your role as the manager should change. You have suspicions in this regard because some of that change has been forced on you, and you will know for sure that it's true if you examine the source of some of your frustrations: what you should be doing, how you wish people were more responsible, and what kind of accountability you long for in the people you manage.

TRANSITIONS

Looking at this from another perspective, you started your career as a doer. You may have even founded a firm in that role, since there weren't enough bodies to require your full time supervision. All this was probably welcome to you, since your training related to the doer role, and that's where you were most comfortable. In this role you touched the work directly; there was nothing between you and the work.

At a certain point you were forced into or willingly embraced the role of manager. In this role you touched the people who did the work. The people you managed stood between you and the work, and your role was not to do the work but to manage the people who did the work.

Most of you are bouncing back and forth between these first two levels, the extent of which is determined by how large your firm is, as well as how much of a control freak you are. The right mix (30/70? 40/60? 75/25?) is difficult to set without knowing more about each of your situations, but since you are entrepreneurs (or technicians who have suffered an entrepreneurial seizure, as Michael Gerber would say), your tendency is always going to be doing more than managing (until you hit a certain stage and embrace the management role more fully).

Ideally, of course, you'll rise to that third and final level: leading. In this role you see and manage the big picture, and most of your efforts are designed to position the department or the firm well and, in this context, to develop the processes that the managers will use to superintend those who are doing.

GROWING TOO FAST

One thing we know is that poorly structured roles are one good indicator that you've been growing too quickly or growing without a plan. In fact, there are many telltale signs that could suggest you have been "letting growth happen to you" rather than pursuing it purposefully, in a controlled manner.

First, are you deadline driven? In these situations, more attention is paid to when things are due than to how many hours are being expended against the budgeted hours.

Second, is budget management still decentralized? If budget management is centralized, you can ask everyone in your office who is responsible for it, and the answer would be consistent. Otherwise they'll say they are, those managing client relationships are, no one is, etc.

Third, do you underestimate your monthly overhead? In situations where growth is too aggressive, it's not infrequent for those in charge to not really know what their "monthly nut" is because their perception has not kept pace with reality.

Fourth, is your cash cushion too thin? If you don't have two to four months set aside, you might be getting too far ahead of your supply wagons.

Fifth, do you have too much turnover? It could be because employees aren't getting what they need. Everybody is doing and too few people are managing.

Sixth, is your workflow cataloged orally? Mature work environments have a written culture that eliminates unnecessary interaction and the inevitable mistakes that arise from it.

Seventh, are your employees complaining from a lack of structure and policy? As we'll discuss below, employees often want more structure than you think they do.

Eighth, does everybody do everything without specific individual responsibility for significant functions? It's a romantic idea to have willing generalists who don't mind pitching in on any task, but it's a tiring way to run a business.

OPTIONS BEFORE GROWTH

So you can see the theme we're developing here: "don't let growth happen to you." This argues for a certain intentionality about growth, which can start by walking yourself through the following checklist. Before you embrace growth (defined as adding bodies), make sure you've walked this path.

Dismiss Clients. Cycling clients is a good thing, because it can allow you to replace marginal clients with more valuable ones. You can spot the more valuable clients because they are more comfortable paying fair prices, they listen to your advice, and they are enjoyable to be around. Clients that should be dismissed often account for a disproportionate amount of your lack of enjoyment and profit. So never grow unless all your clients are good ones.

Raise Prices. As the currency of respect, money is a useful way to filter good clients from bad. If you are charging for enough of your time, try charging for the same percentage at a higher hourly rate. If you need to charge more, raising prices will inevitably slim down your client base, leaving more room for those new clients on the roster. So never grow until your current clients are paying fair prices.

Outsource. How do you know that this increased volume of work will be sustained? It's easier for a client to trim their requests than it is for you to trim your staff. Until you are sure that the change is permanent, use variable sources, such as independent professionals, formerly called freelancers. Deciding to not use them as much is less emotional than dismissing staff. So never grow until you are confident that the new work level is sustainable enough to hire.

Resist Overreaching. Many firms believe that they don't dare let another firm dance with the girl they brought to the party, so they say "yes" to projects that they cannot do profitably and which often are outside their expertise. This probably stems from an insecurity in the relationship, fearing that the client will fall in love with the alternate provider and edge them out. Come on, folks. Do what you do best, and think of the client's best interest. Once you taste a competent relationship, you'll never go back. So never grow until you are only doing the things that you are really good at.

Ensure Cash Funding. Ready access to credit makes it too easy to grow. This natural filter that used to be in the marketplace is less prevalent as credit sources (leases or loans) abound to give you most anything you want, regardless of whether it's good for you. This is a huge mistake on their part and yours. Fund growth with cash, not only because it slows you down, but because there'll be less of a mess to clean up if you blow it. So never grow unless you can fund the growth with cash.

Accept Role Change. Finally, you are ready to think about the biggest issue when it comes to growth. Are you ready to accept and even embrace a different role? You might even pass the first five tests, but that's not enough. You must pass all six tests. The last question is the most important one. So never grow unless you are willing to slide further away from "doing" and further toward "managing."

Let's talk about how to put a plan together that does just that.

GROWING WITH A PLAN

Focused Roles. Appropriate structure is relative. The fact that it's not working now does not mean that it was not appropriate at one point. In other words, what might have worked when you had fewer people might not be a good choice now. The first mistake managers make when adding staff is to add people who can "help get things off my plate." The impetus, of course, is that they are a bottleneck, having to touch far too many things, giving scant attention to all. By hiring someone to assist with this, the problem will get worse because now there is an expectation that the manager has even greater capacity with this new help. But everything still has to go through him or her, slowing the process down even further.

This hiring mistake can be brought about by not having much money, and thus only being able to hire a lower level employee who cannot do anything but help an experienced one.

What happens when this hiring method is followed? You'll have the top people getting more and more frazzled, little initiative in the ranks, and an unclear sense of who's responsible for what. And you'll be doing incompetent work unless you touch it personally—and even then it might be incompetent.

So start to focus the roles. Regardless of the stated reasons for not doing so, the real reason for this hiring method is insecurity.

Expert Hires. You need to hire people who do one or a few things really well. Ask yourself: "Am I hiring this employee because they can teach us something? Because they can perform a particular function better than anybody else currently on staff?" If you can't answer "yes" to these two questions, pause and think carefully about the strategy. (Note that this mistake often masks itself as the desire to hire people you can train, who can learn the way you do things.)

Here's another question. Can you step into nearly any position and do it as well or better than the employee now charged with that role? Shame on you. You've hired far too low, and subconsciously you've done it because you did not want to cede control to someone else. If you are content with the way things are, there's no problem with that strategy, except this: your firm will never rise above your own competence. That might or might not be scary, depending on how competent you are. Time for a change, maybe.

Need vs. Afford. Another one of those habits that's hard to break is hiring people based on what you can afford. Now, that's a prudent step at the beginning when competence isn't that critical. But stick with that plan later, and you'll cycle too many employees looking for ones that really contribute, and are willing to do so at less than market value.

A better plan is to determine what competence you can't afford to be without. At this stage, you may even be able to hire one good person to replace two less able ones who might not be a good fit for where you are now.

Here's a note of caution. When you hire that first person who's going to make more than you've usually been paying, your expectations will be so high that you might create an environment that is unfair to that new employee, and then write them off sooner than you should. At the second hire, though, your expectations will be informed more by how the first hire failed, and the match might be better. (As in any battle, the first person into the breach usually gets killed.)

Role Exchange. Finally, in smaller firms where everybody must wear more than one hat, at least be sure you know what hat is being worn. In other words, function like a bigger firm so that you'll be ready to slide into that mode when your employee numbers allow it. There's another reason, too, why you should be aware of which hat you are wearing: it facilitates the transfer of that function later because you'll be able to separate your activities by function.

WHAT THIS MEANS

This brings us back to the issue of structure. That's what growth means. It means that your structure—and particularly your personal role—must change and adapt to a new way of managing.

Lack of structure, or an improper structure, obviously has implications. The first thing you'll find is that too little role definition translates into too little responsibility (and a resulting lack of quality)! In other words, things won't get done because it won't be clear who is responsible. And once you notice that they are not getting done, you won't be sure who to admonish, either.

The second thing you'll notice is less staff satisfaction than there should be. Of course there could be many reasons for this, but in this context the reason is simple. Employees typically define their own significance by what they do, and without a clear (job) description of what they do, it's difficult for them to find a place for themselves. In fact, if you don't help them understand how they fit into the structure, they will find their significance in other ways, some of which are destructive. For example, instead of defining their significance by their focused expertise, they might define it by how many different things they have done over the years or by their relationship to you, personally.

The third thing you'll notice is your own personal burnout. This comes from having too many things on your plate (frazzled neurons) and being too integral to the process to be able to take extended breaks.

Of course you know all these things, because you have experienced them in some form. The point is that they come from lack of structure, primarily. (Lack of systems can contribute to the issue, but that's another subject.)

DANGERS OF AVOIDING STRUCTURE

Many enterprises have let structure just appear over time, feeling a little powerless to make it happen. It's a reactive process. Others have intentionally resisted it.

Either way, there are real dangers in avoiding structure, whether it's this kind of structure or your own brand of it. Here are some thoughts on that subject.

Confused Employees. When you started your firm, one of the early vows was that you'd forego much of the structure that you so despised at the larger firm you left. If this hasn't happened already, you'll soon learn that employees are not like you or they'd be running their own firms. They want more structure than you think they do.

Less Contribution. If you don't have a clearly defined place to plug people in, you'll hire generalists with great attitudes and then expect them to jump around doing anything that's needed. You'll appreciate them, but they won't move your firm forward.

Too Much Training. If you hire these generalists, you'll waste an inordinate amount of time training them. In fact, you might even need to do it yourself, since you know more about how things should be done than anyone else.

Mind Always Running. Unless you have competent people who know what they should be doing, your mind will always be occupied trying to remember details.

Misplaced Significance. People must find significance in some way. If you don't supply it to them via a job description (where the sandbox boundaries are defined and they get credit for anything that's built inside that box), they'll turn to less productive ways to "be significant." Namely, they'll define their significance in terms of how close their relationship is with you, always talking about your favor to them, about how long they've been there, and how many different ways they've contributed.

No Extended Departures. Want to take more time off? Get your structure fixed so you are less essential on a daily basis but more essential in the bigger picture.

Difficult Transitions. What's going to happen to your enterprise after you leave? Ideally, a new manager can step in and manage the very capable people you had put in place. But if too much depends on you personally, transitions are difficult.

Now let's take a look at structuring your own priorities on the job.

YOUR OWN PRIORITIES

I'd like to focus on the priorities that principals and managers should follow as they lead the enterprise. Without a single exception, there are five priorities for where to focus. But it's not just the list that's important—the sequence is also in a very specific order. You make sure you're doing the first one, and if that's all you have time to do, then so be it. But if you are doing the first one well, you can and should advance to the second priority. And so on, until there is no more time or energy left.

No. 1: Minding the Financial Performance. Your first priority as a principal or manager is to pilot the ship. That means ensuring accurate tracking of your firm or department's financial performance against industry benchmarks, useful forecasting, and prudent decisions about the source and use of money. Armed with that information, you will make good decisions about staffing, benefits, facility, miscellaneous overhead, and the use of outside resources. Other people can help you do all this, but your finger must be on the financial pulse of the firm.

No. 2: Hiring/Molding Key Staff. There's been a shift over the past few years to the point where it's actually more difficult to find the right people than the right clients. It follows, of course, that there's more at stake when you make a mistake with employees than with clients. All that to say that you need a marketing plan for attracting staff to yield so many candidates that you can be picky, finding that influential person with the right talent and perspective on the working culture of your firm.

If you are currently spending your time taking care of clients, you're on an endless treadmill which will keep you running until you're so tired that you collapse and fall off. You're solving the same problems every day, and growth will only exacerbate the problem.

Of course, a major portion of your effectiveness in managing these key people will depend on hiring the right ones in the first place. So before you write the marketing plan for staff, start with the right positioning: crafting a place where great people want to work, in part because you're there shaping them.

By the way, if you aren't sure who is in this group, consider that you should not have more than six or eight people or so reporting to you. That's the group we're talking about.

No. 3: Positioning/Closing Opportunity. Once you've nailed those two things, it's time to make sure your firm or department has a very clear and differentiated positioning in the marketplace, built around deep expertise that's different from nearly every one of your peer firms or departments. Even though that task is critical, it is not time-consuming, and you don't need to revisit it except every few years.

From there, it's important that you have a presence in the process of closing opportunity (i.e., making clients out of prospects). You don't need to orchestrate that process, but the prospect should register the fact that you've shown your face, complimented the team that will serve them, and described the culture of your firm, their new partner.

These three may be as far as you need to go, but if you still have time and energy left, add the next two, in order.

No. 4: Strategizing for Clients. You've been doing this for years (standing "naked" in front of prospects and clients, thinking on your feet), guiding recommendations to clients from your acquired expertise. The best way to be involved with clients without being their daily go-to person is to bounce in and out of the relationship while you help them formulate the strategic portion of the marketing plan for their product or service.

Clients will be grateful for your attention, and your employees will soak up the shared knowledge that's imparted in the process.

No. 5: Implementing for Clients. If you're managing the first four priorities like you should, there's virtually no chance that you'll have time for client implementation work. But if you do, you'll probably be doing the same things that got you into the field in the first place.

Whatever that is, it's implementation (and likely a waste of your abilities). But never dip your toes in those waters again unless you're doing a terrific job with the first four priorities.

FINALLY

If there's more than one of you running the enterprise, you can enjoy one of the few advantages of a partnership: splitting up the responsibilities and focusing deeper in the process.

Otherwise, use this checklist to make sure you're being the manager your enterprise needs.

Next, let's look at some basic tenets of managing well.

11

Managing Right

This chapter discusses the type of environment in which employees thrive. We've already covered some of these elements, but I want to put them all together in one place.

I'll begin by noting why this is important, and then explain how your role as a manager fits into the overall picture. Against the grayness of management, black and white decisions must be made, and that's your role. If you aren't managing, or if you just aren't suited for it, the evidence will be all over your firm or department. Based on thousands of surveys and follow-up interviews, this chapter provides more than seventy-five suggestions about what employees appreciate in the working environment, organized into categories: hiring, integration, structure, performance, workload, environment, communications, support, personal, conflicts of interest, external respect, and exiting.

THE BENEFITS OF EMPLOYEES WHO ARE CONTENT

The context of this discussion is creating an environment where employees want to work, which will obviously have far reaching implications. First, as prospective employees hear about your environment, they'll be favorably swayed to join you. Second, once they do join, they'll be more likely to stay. Third, they'll consistently do better work for your clients because valuable mental energy is not being used on protecting their own interests. Fourth, you'll sleep better at night, especially through the tough times, knowing you are doing the right thing.

YOUR ROLE AS MANAGER

If you are the designated manager, you must manage. The business or department you run is a direct reflection of you, which can be a terrifying or invigorating concept.

Of course you can delegate certain functions of employee management (like tracking vacation days), but everyone will follow your lead in how employees are valued...and thus how they are treated. This will happen in spite of any layer you might place between yourself and employees. Layers will not effectively insulate you from shaping the management environment, since all employees will look beyond the layer to you, the tone-setter.

THE GRAYNESS OF MANAGEMENT

Managing people is the most personally painful thing you do. Sure, establishing systems is perplexing, but the implications of failure are more mental and financial, not personal or ethical. The management environment, though, is a complex task always out of reach. And worst of all, it seldom moves from gray into black and white. It's hard to know that you've done the right thing, and doing the right thing is a deeper concern in this arena than your other areas of responsibility. Or at least it should be.

We make time for the things we enjoy. We defer the things we don't. For most principals and even some managers, managing people fits into the latter category.

We make time for the things we enjoy. We enjoy the things we are good at. This is true of sports, vocation, and management ability. But unfortunately, choosing to grow is an unwitting (and often unfulfilled) commitment to managing more and doing less. This chapter is about creating an environment where employees want to work, which is just one small facet of your management responsibility.

THE BASIS FOR THIS CHAPTER

Since 1994 I have spent one to two days on an individual basis with more than seventy principals and key managers every year. A few of those have been a little paranoid, self-absorbed, and mean-spirited. But the vast majority are delightful, smart, hard-working individuals trying to find their way and struggling to adapt to a management role for which they have had no training and few mentors indeed.

In working with them, I have surveyed thousands of their employees, as well. Following the confidential written survey, each employee has been interviewed for twenty to thirty minutes in person, on-site. This chapter is a compilation of the things that repeatedly surface, as well as my suggestions on how to create an environment conducive to satisfied employees (and managers).

Here is what your employees are saying to you. Or rather what your best employees would say to you in a moment of honest feedback. I'll phrase things from their perspective.

HIRING

Avoid hinting at things during the interview that might be interpreted as certainties, like a retirement plan soon to be implemented, or the possibility of sharing ownership in the firm. Only talk about things that are certain but just not implemented, or I will later feel cheated when they don't come to pass.

Make a prompt decision (either yes or no) about hiring me. Drawn out decisions are frustrating to me, the applicant, and make me question the importance of the role I'll have.

But be thorough in the hiring process, since that communicates that you have been thorough in other hires, making it less likely that bad choices are still on staff.

Provide me with a clear explanation of my role, in writing, and consult with me first before making any substantive changes.

Delineate your expectations of this position, also in writing. Being clear is more respectful than letting assumptions rule.

INTEGRATION

Don't let my entrance serve as the announcement that someone has been hired. Keep my fellow employees informed.

Have a place for me to work with all the basics there.

Use a fixed orientation procedure, dividing the checklist between several employees who will each spend some time explaining how things are done, giving me a chance to get to know several people at the outset.

Ask me to share my early perspectives. They might be more valuable at the beginning before I get used to the way things are done. These can be stored in a log of first impressions and then shared later when I'm more confident in how the suggestions will be received.

Give me time to adjust to a new work environment, trimming your expectations for the first month or two.

STRUCTURE

I want one supervisor, not several. This manager should be the same person responsible for my performance reviews, setting my salary, and hiring/dismissing me. Or at least they should make final recommendations to a principal in that regard.

Provide a written job description, preferably with my input.

Describe a career path, where possible, that helps me see where I can move next, particularly if I wish to assume added responsibility.

Determine and communicate a rough salary range for my position, explaining that compensation outside that range is possible if the firm grows and/or if I demonstrate a strong aptitude for a position with a higher salary range.

PERFORMANCE

Provide unprompted reviews of my performance at least yearly, in writing. Don't force me to remind you that it's due, and then don't keep deferring the meeting.

Meet with me monthly, even for just a half hour, to discuss mutual performance, not projects. Base the discussion on simple notes each of us has taken since the last meeting. Of course a more formal review every year is important, too.

Keep me busy with productive assignments. I am most content when I am making a valuable contribution.

WORKLOAD

Create a sustainable work environment where, on average, I don't work more than forty-five hours per week.

Be fair about comp time, providing as much flexibility when I want off as you expect me to provide when something unusual needs to be done.

Let me concentrate without too many interruptions. When what I am doing is less important than getting something off your mind, a certain lack of respect is communicated about my schedule in relation to yours.

Ask that work requests be filtered through my supervisor, who will balance competing requests and protect me from unreasonable expectations.

Seek my approval before pledging after hours work on my behalf for a client.

Protect my chance to take a mid-day meal break, and I'll be willing to work while I eat on rare occasions when it is necessary.

Allow me some degree of flexibility about schedule, especially when my normal hours begin and end (e.g., to miss rush hour traffic). But then expect me to follow the plan consistently.

Manage situations where demand exceeds supply, either using outside contractors, hiring new employees who can contribute quickly, or just saying no.

Give all of us a chance to work on the best projects.

ENVIRONMENT

Use the appropriate form of communication, handling tough issues in person, not through email.

Paint the parameters for my job and then let me really contribute instead of expecting me to simply implement your ideas.

Sell my ideas hard, or at least expect me to give you the ammunition to do so.

Let us collaborate as employees, and be willing to reflect that fact in budgets presented to clients.

A comfortable chair is worth it. Spend what it takes to get me one.

Provide me with a training budget, and then expect me to use it, reporting on the experience when I return so that others can learn too.

Solicit my feedback on the benefit structure, listening carefully for what would be useful for my situation.

Organize social events so that we can spend time together apart from deadlines.

Let me take the spotlight, during and after projects.

Don't hire losers I'll have to work with.

Occasionally let us do a cool, money-losing project just for fun, especially if we've been responsible about making lots of money for you on other work.

Don't enable me by stepping in all the time with a rescue plan.

Treat us all fairly, but don't treat us all the same. Don't discriminate, but do be distinct in singling me and others out when the situation warrants it.

COMMUNICATIONS

Put things in writing and take the time to tell me everything I need to know up front. Dribbling out just enough information to get me started only communicates that you don't have time for me or trust me, since it keeps you inevitably in the loop.

Tell me what I need to know, but no more. I'm uncomfortable knowing what other people make, what personal problems you are struggling with, and how a particular employee is doing poorly.

Tell us where the company is going from a larger perspective. There's a lot at stake here for us, too, and we love knowing that you are taking the time to think and plan.

SUPPORT

Get the full story before passing judgment on my actions. Sometimes my fellow employees have agendas of their own, and you should be able to sort those out.

Give me your priority time, not what's left over.

Show random appreciation for what I do. It tells me that I matter in the scheme of things.

PERSONAL

I want to respect you as a person of integrity. This is fundamental.

Any time you spend planning the course of this business will be welcome. If you are doing more than managing, I'm worried about who's steering this ship.

Keep your emotional and sexual attractions in check. It will cloud the management environment and destroy the fabric of how we relate to each other.

Follow the policies yourself so that I can see how serious you are about system wide institutionalization.

Don't cling to your own status, but don't work too hard at artificially leveling your position, either. In other words, if you need a private office, I'll understand. You aren't one of us and shouldn't try to act like it.

Don't be afraid of us lest we lose respect for you. We are okay with you making mistakes, but we are not okay with you not taking risks.

Don't be afraid of conflict or sweep it under the rug. Conflict is inevitable and that's when we need you the most.

Have a life outside work and don't be embarrassed about it.

Don't expect me to be as committed as a shareholder would be. I don't have as much at stake as you do, and I want a life outside work, too. That's why I'm working for you and not myself.

Don't avoid management decisions by enacting extensive regulations, like using a handbook that attempts to address every possible situation.

Quit waffling—just go ahead and fire that person. We all know it needs to happen.

And go ahead and tell them when you've made the decision instead of just not looking at them anymore!

Don't appeal to loyalty when you want me to stay late or turn down that job offer. Let's keep our accounts short: you pay me fairly and I'll give you value. We should both be able to walk away from this without owing each other anything.

Take extended time off so that we can show you how much we really don't need you around to run this place well.

Separate the business from yourself, giving both you and me freedom to critique it meaningfully without defensiveness on your part.

CONFLICTS OF INTEREST

Hire people because of their skill, not because they are your friends or relatives. It's okay to hire friends and relatives, but we'll be suspicious and their skill level will be even more critical (for their credibility and yours).

Don't single people out for your favor by spending inordinate amounts of time with them, especially outside work. I'll question whether that will favor their chances for advancement, plum assignments, and special treatment.

I don't necessarily want to be your friend, but I do want to enjoy working with you.

Make good business decisions that are good for the group, not ones that are unduly influenced by your personal interests, such as clients you like, unprofitable projects that you believe in, connected community leaders you might be afraid of saying "no" to, etc.

EXTERNAL RESPECT

Don't over-service clients. Let's make each of them pay their way, and let's stand up to them when they ask too much. Over-servicing usually has implications for us, too.

Ask how effective our work is for clients, and then share those results with us. We feel attached to the work we do, and want to be aware of the impact we are having.

Don't price our work too low. That's motivated by your lack of confidence personally, or lack of confidence in us. Either way we are making an expensive mistake. Listen to us about what it's worth—we have less at stake financially and will help you set prices that reflect the marketplace, not your natural fears about meeting payroll.

Market our firm aggressively. That communicates your pride in what we do, and it will also give me more to talk about when people ask where I work. I want to be plugged into a firm that is going somewhere.

In that same vein, let us selectively enter award shows. I'll be able to boast to my peers, and you'll find that it's easier to attract other great employees who want to work for a firm they've heard of before.

EXIT

When I leave, ask me why I've made that choice. Be eager to secure my feedback so you can learn from it.

Treat me with respect when I move to another job, particularly if I've been a good employee. My agendas won't necessarily match yours, and I want to experience different environments, maybe even getting out of the box you've built around me. In fact, I might want to come back some day, bringing even more value after I've learned from other good teachers like you.

FINALLY

These should not be viewed as seventy-five ways to make you feel guilty. Most of you are far better at managing than you give yourself credit for.

Leadership is essentially the ability to create, communicate, and motivate toward a vision.

And then it's taking risks. And leading, which are really two words for the same thing.

Now, before we leave this topic entirely, let me offer a suggestion in the next chapter on an alternative to the typical performance review that managers might give.

12

A Performance Review You Might Even Enjoy

There's a problem with the typical annual performance review, and the best evidence of that is the fact that you, the manager, dread doing them or just keep avoiding them entirely. Let me propose a much simpler approach—hundreds of my clients are doing this now and would never go back to the traditional method.

Performance reviews are necessary. They're a critical step in the process of building and maintaining a team. They don't work on their own, though, so you might do better if you consider them as the fifth step in a five-part process of management.

SETTING THE STAGE

First, you need to know what you want from people. That includes skills, attitude, deportment, teamwork, etc. Be very detailed, articulating what's important to you from a staffing standpoint, generally, and then be specific about that position.

Second, find the right person to do it. I don't know what the actual percentage is, but at least eighty percent of a good management experience has to be finding the right person in the first place. Good—even great—management seldom turns a bad employee into a good one.

Third, express your expectations (see the first point, above) to that person in a way that they absorb and understand your intent.

Fourth, reinforce those expectations by your own actions, and by what you say. These are typically teaching moments comprised of a smile or frown at the right time and place, a handwritten note, an email, or whatever flows from who you are. If you took the time to note each teaching moment in a given work day, you'd be able to recall several dozen of them in that one day alone.

Fifth, discuss and tweak performance expectations in a more formal setting, based on the extent to which the employee is demonstrating assent to your expressed description of the culture that you desire. This last element is the performance review, but it must be seen in context. Know what you want, find the right person, make sure they understand what you want, reinforce and model this behavior, and then talk about how well the employee is doing. In a nutshell, that's management.

TYPICAL PERFORMANCE REVIEW

As I noted in opening this chapter, the typical performance review doesn't work, and here are the two reasons why.

First, it's more of a one-way monologue instead of a more appropriate two-way dialogue between you and the employee. It shouldn't be just about how the employee is conforming but also about how you are managing.

Second, it's typically an annual event. That means that the pressure on a specific outcome is heightened, but it also means that the discussion is skewed toward more recent events, which leaves the first portion of the review period unreviewed, so to speak! And because it's common for changes in compensation to also be annual, there's too much happening at an annual review. "If I'm told some tough things in my review, does that mean I won't get much of a raise?" If you uncouple the review from the raise by doing the former more frequently, bad news is easier to accept.

A WORTHWHILE ALTERNATIVE: TWENTY-MINUTE WALK

I've discovered, as have hundreds of my clients, that there's a better way to do this—a way that addresses all the downsides of a traditional annual performance review and builds some entirely new features into the process. Let me describe it with one paragraph, and then we'll look at all the elements, each of which is important to enable great success.

The alternative is a monthly, twenty-minute mutual performance discussion walk, based on a monthly log. It is unscheduled but callable by either party.

Now for the explanation of each element.

First, doing it monthly is about right. There's not enough to talk about if you do it weekly and all the events of the period aren't fresh if you do it quarterly.

Second, spending twenty minutes is about right. It's not long enough to really cramp anything else you might need to do that day, but it does provide plenty of time to plant seeds and suggest actions.

Third, it's about mutual performance in more of a two-way dialogue than a one-way monologue (thus the word discussion). In fact, occasionally include the manager's manager or someone the employee manages for a three-way conversation.

Fourth, always do it on a walk. It's easier to say things when there's built-in action that doesn't require thought to undertake, like walking. It's also easier when you can look at each other occasionally instead of all the time. Maybe best of all, it gets you both out of the office in a fresh setting, all without the distractions that pervade the office environment.

Fifth, the conversation follows the outline provided in the monthly log. This prevents awkward silences and manufactured conversation. Instead, you're talking about goals, slips in performance, great wins, examples of expressed gratitude, etc. The log helps you remember and even capture the emotion of a particular event. But you don't have to actually talk about it right then, which allows for the passage of time—the best antidote to saying something regretful or outside a broader context.

Sixth, you don't want to schedule these far in advance and thus set the stage for a mere twenty-minute event to keep getting rescheduled. No, we don't have to schedule the things that are important to us, and these should fit into that category. This will be something you want to do, and either one of you can go to the other and say: "Hey, is this a good time for our monthly connection?" If it is, both of you grab the logs and off you go. Continually rescheduling an event like a performance review communicates lack of interest, comfort, or care, and none of those are good.

FINALLY

So, what becomes of the yearly performance review? Hold it, still, but make it a compilation, review, and even a celebration of progress.

If this is something that interests you, let me suggest that you just explain it as a one-month trial. Don't make a big announcement. Instead, do the first one, see if you and the employees in your care get hooked, and then just keep doing them.

Now that we've looked at some very specific things employees want from you, let's talk about the softer, less-defined side of leadership. That is, what sort of leaders are they going to want to follow.

13

Moving Beyond
Reluctant Leadership

I suppose it should come as no surprise that statistically most of us are not leaders. Though running a business or managing a department, does tend to force the issue a bit, creating unwitting leaders of many of us.

Being a leader is tantamount to being a risk taker, which is essentially the same thing as being an entrepreneur. But they are very different risks. Borrowing money, signing your name to big documents, and promising clients outlandish things is what entrepreneurs do and call it risky. But sitting down with that attitude-challenged employee, deciding on bonuses, or sifting through resumes is where the real risks lie. Palpitation is the order of the day. They say that fear of public speaking tops our list of phobias. I would respectfully submit that a fear of managing people is nearer the top.

I spoke at a conference one time and unwittingly tricked people with a title. I say unwittingly because I believe that truth in advertising is particularly appropriate when titling presentations, lest attendees vote with their feet and leave within a few minutes. This presentation was mistakenly entitled "Insulating Yourself from Management." As I discovered later, the title itself was a huge draw, because managers the world over are looking for ways to get out of it. Out of managing, that is. The benefits of management (prestige, control, money) are enough to keep them managing so that employment remains intact, but there are parts of their lives they would gladly give up and management is at the top of that list.

My perspective is that management is more about making distinguishing decisions in an environment not conducive to it than it is about putting systems in place that effectively self-manage people. If self-management were effective, a lot of you would be less grumpy, and unless we recognize our tendency to insulate ourselves from the down and dirty side of management, we will waste precious effort on systems that are doomed to fail from the start.

Think for a second about insulation. The more effectively certain products insulate, the more consumers are willing to pay for them. The "R" value of home insulation, the mug that is still steaming when you pull into the parking lot, the airliner with engines that just seem to turn without any sound. All of these products are valuable.

Many of our management practices, too, are meant to insulate us from the need to manage. They are disguised as "good management" when in fact they are not. For example, we create over-complicated employee manuals so that we can point to a page when any question surfaces. Or we install a simple formula for bonuses and invoke it once a year just before Christmas.

We don't dare think of this as a great way to manage people. Distinguishing decisions are the choices you make about how well people are living up to their potential, or where your enterprise should head in the future, or what risk to take on when choosing that new direction, or what kind of employee to hire. If you are typical, you have a sense about where to head with each decision, but fear of some sort is holding you back. But not trusting your instincts leads to inaction, a choice—and yes it is a choice—typically worse than the wrong but more proactive choice.

You cannot work too hard to avoid the inevitable grayness otherwise called management. Instead, you should be trying to do the right thing, looking for ways to clarify your own plans for this group of people. After all that deliberation, in the end you must step back and do it because it's the right thing. Or at least because you think it might be, which could very well be as much certainty as you'll get.

THE TOUGH ODDS

Several things contribute to make this struggle particularly acute.

First, the enterprises we manage are typically small, and so there is little moving up the ranks, learning skills in a measured, safer way with fewer victims to litter the path. Instead, one day you are just managing, quickly trying to catch up with yourself.

Second, our educations are technical, not managerial. It would not be typical to attend a single class on how to manage people. This is changing slowly, thankfully, but we are decades away from a rounded curriculum that mirrors real life experience in managing.

Third, small enterprises are highly fragmented within their industries, spurning peer learning, honest collaboration, and management mentoring. The world is our playground, so to speak, and so there are competitors behind every stone. There is a bravado in going it alone, a fierce sense of confidentiality, and a reticence or even deep fear of exposing our struggles. Think for a moment about the silly posturing that consumes industry events. Two principals meeting for the first time will try, as quickly as possible, to size up the other by determining number of employees, awards won, and presence of substantial clients. All this somehow is a substitute for how much money someone makes or how soon they go home at night. As prototypical managers we are, frankly, bored with people who are normal, who manage well, and who live balanced lives.

Fourth, it's not too hard to just give up and quit fighting. These businesses you are in are tough, and that involves a certain amount of struggle with clients. Not enough energy remains to struggle with employees, too. So we just do the minimum and hope the problems will sink back below the surface, to be handled another day, or forgotten altogether.

Fifth, our society rewards non-confrontational individuals. Management is about confrontation, not in a mean-spirited way, but confrontation nonetheless. Management is either seeing the potential for something headed in the wrong direction or actually seeing it happen. Either way, a manager must step in and gently (at a minimum) wrest control from momentum and lead with intention.

IT'S STILL YOUR JOB

As tempting as it might be, though, managing people is one of those things you can never delegate. That alone might keep you up at night. I have interviewed hundreds of principals since 1994, asking for their feedback. One of the questions I have specifically asked is "What frustrates you?" Listen to two different but typical responses:

"My least favorite part is HR. In a small company, it's very hard to be objective. I hate dealing with employees on salary issues because I never know what's reasonable. Even though I've developed a good system for performance evaluations, I dislike communicating the negative. I hate having to micro-manage bad behavior, and until recently, have often ignored it hoping it would just go away."

Here's another:

"What frustrates me? Keeping people accountable. The staff not carrying through on their commitments, dropping details, or mismanaging under the name of creative freedom. I also struggle with their poor planning and time management, creating self imposed restrictions on the potential of the project. I dislike not being able to extract myself from the "client confidence building" role, as well as the unending and moving-target nature of addressing creative staffing needs. I also don't know when to support and listen and when to draw the line and stand firm, and I wish I could establish a correlation between the business aspects of design and the creative aspects of design."

Neither of these folks would get up in the morning, eager to tackle these problems. They are speed bumps on the way to doing what they really want to do, like land big clients or tackle the big problems those clients have.

MANAGEMENT IS PRACTICED

We make time for the things we enjoy. We defer the things we don't. For most managers, managing people fits into the latter category. But after all is said and done, management is really listening, being decisive, pulling yourself out of the details so that management happens, making distinguishing decisions, etc. It's not like running a nuclear reactor, where lots of instruction is essential ahead of time. It's more like learning to throw a Frisbee. If you want to improve, the key is to do it, listening to a few principles in the background as you trim the trees with those initially errant shots. Here are a few of those principles.

First, just do it. Unhealthy management environments are marked by managers who are doing the work of the firm instead of managing the people of the firm. It's not that they are bad managers but rather that they aren't managing. No one is steering the ship, charting a course, or providing direction. You are a better manager than you think. Just start doing it, exercising your management muscle before it turns to fat.

Second, get a therapist. Any personal struggles will boil over into your management experience. If you are struggling with your personal significance, intent on controlling every aspect of life, or highly fearful of confrontation, working through those issues will be time well spent.

I remember sitting with two married principals of a twenty-five person firm. During the debriefing process, I looked to the woman, and with my pulse racing offered this feedback: "The employees find you intimidating and harsh. Because of that, you are having trouble coaxing them. They are hurting after their interactions with you, and feeling dispirited." She reacted very strongly and claimed to not see it at all. She didn't understand how anybody could feel that way. I added that I could understand, because I was feeling the same way, and I was not someone who was easily intimidated!

The meeting went on for another hour, during which she said very little, and I admired my own foresight in getting a rental car so that I wouldn't have to walk to the airport. I packed up and began to leave the conference room. She asked if she could walk me to the parking garage. I gulped and said yes, wishing I had written a farewell note to my family and hidden it somewhere on my body.

We walked for three blocks before anything happened. Then she began to cry very quietly and said: "You're right. Thanks for having the courage to say something." She turned around without saying another word, and we parted ways. I never spoke with her again.

I didn't want to say anything to her, and I wasn't sure I had all the facts straight. But to go back to the first point, you must act before you are certain or you will always wait too long. Certainty is not a luxury you have when it comes to management, and chasing it will lead to analysis-paralysis on your part. I acted before I was certain and that decision had great impact.

Third, get a life. Quit trying to please everyone, particularly employees. Don't be afraid of them. Find cheaper ways to make friends. Make work only a small portion of your life so that you can put it into perspective and not become a hostage.

Most of you are looking for the wrong things from your job. Almost all of you are afflicted with S.D.D. (stimulation deficit disorder), compounded by a nearly constitutional belief that you have the right to find the cure in your work. We'll talk more about that later in the chapter on work/life balance.

Fourth, articulate your personal vision. What do you want to do when you grow up? How does your current role fit into that plan? How does that translate into a certain necessary level of management on your part to get to that point?

It's a sloppy process, but hang in there. Be honest with yourself and then courageous about the choices that surface. Leadership is really about having the courage to act on your instincts, after which other doors will open for you and you'll see things that were not available to you in the past.

As I noted earlier, management is really listening, being decisive, pulling yourself out of the details so that management happens, making distinguishing decisions, etc.

Bad managers who don't want to improve will get worse as time passes, but bad managers who want to improve actually do so. That's probably why effective managers tend to be confident, humble, and patient.

True leadership is always mixed with some reluctance because it's always messy. But you must move beyond your reluctance to lead, recognizing that you'll never shed that reluctance that properly comes from wanting to know you've done the right thing.

Let's look next at the specific qualities of a leader that employees would like to follow.

14

Being a Leader
They Want to Follow

In the last chapter, we talked about what it means to move beyond reluctant leadership. We didn't look at what that leadership looks like, though, and that's what I'd like to do in this chapter. Well, really I'd like to talk about what that leader looks like.

What are the characteristics of a leader who others want to follow? As you'll soon see, this list is a very personal one. In other words, we'd all come up with different elements when building the list. What I've tried to do, though, is to think of a complete leader. So I've asked myself this question: can I imagine a leader who isn't fair, for instance. The answer is obviously no.

Each one of these, then, describes a leader's characteristics, any one of which might hinder their effectiveness if missing in any significant proportion. What I'd encourage you to do—maybe even before you read this list—is to first make up your own list and compare it with mine. These are not presented in any particular order.

APPROACHABLE

A leader, who is really nothing more than the ideal form of a manager, is approachable, even with bad news. There's an evenness and steadiness that gives those who must approach him or her a confidence that they won't be yelled at or blamed unnecessarily.

At the heart of approachability is simply a willingness to listen, first, before reacting to a particular piece of news.

ARTICULATE

A leader doesn't need to be some master spokesperson or have a Ph.D. in English, but they need to be able to articulate what they are thinking and feeling. A vision is not that useful unless it can be imparted to the others who will join along in that journey.

It's not just the words, either, but the tone and the speech patterns and the actual words that are chosen. You might say that a leader doesn't have to be articulate, but they do need to articulate.

I'll never forget leading a seminar and positing that everybody involved in account service must be articulant. I said it that way and then misspelled it on the flip chart! So that's not what I'm talking about, here. Mistakes are okay, but the point is that a leader should be able to express a concept as a necessary step in building consensus around it.

AUTHENTIC

A leader needs to be the same person on the surface as they are in reality, deep inside. Employees can smell a rat, and that rat often takes the form of a leader who dons a suit when at work, trying to be somebody they aren't.

The opposite of authentic is fake, and that fakeness can be manifested in the form of fake friendship, fake listening, fake humor, fake caring, etc. Real leaders are the same person at work as they might be if you bump into them at the grocery store.

COMMUNICATIVE

Not only are leaders able to articulate their vision, they actually do so. That's what I mean by communicative. They frequently impact the environment by speaking to it. They are present and involved and know what they want, communicating that in ways that make a favorable impression on those they depend on to get the work done.

COMPETENT AT A BASIC LEVEL

Leaders need a basic level of competence. Just enough to understand the issues and be able to evaluate talent. They should not, however, be the most technically competent of the group. If they are, that may be a sign that they have hired helpers instead of experts. It could also mean that they were promoted for the wrong reasons (the best doer rather than the best manager).

Let's face it: all over the world you can find well-run companies whose leaders are managing others who are far more competent than they are.

CONFIDENT

Leaders are confident, but this is a tough characteristic to describe with balance. That's because there's always a fair measure of self-doubt with leadership. On the other end of the spectrum, too little confidence makes for ineffective leadership. So there's a balance somewhere in there: enough confidence to inspire those following a leader, but not so much confidence that it leads them astray.

CURIOUS

There are many words I could have used for this component of a leader, but curiosity is critical. Closely aligned with this would be perceptive, observant, and inquiring. All these attributes are utilized with a view toward the possibility that the leader is wrong. He or she holds a belief, but is always testing it against new information in new situations to further refine their learning and thus their convictions. They are always on the hunt for new perspectives that can be brought to bear on their management.

DECISION MAKER

Leaders who take too long to make decisions, or don't make them decisively enough, are bound to struggle. To be an effective leader you must be a risk taker. In chaos and ambiguity, you must defy momentum and decide about direction and speed. It's fine—and even desirable—to tolerate ambiguity, but that analog environment cannot prevent digital decisions from being made.

DIRECT

Leaders are direct. Not rude, but direct. The difference lies in the intent and result. Being direct is motivated by a desire to truly communicate in a means whereby everything that's necessary is included without any ancillary information or clutter. Hurting someone with directness is an example of poor leadership because it gets in the way of good, honest communication.

Leaders are direct so that there's no confusion about what's being said or what's behind it.

DISCIPLINED

Leaders are disciplined. That means that they get things done, do what they say, plan, and execute. They can set goals, control their actions, and systematically work toward a set of accomplishments. It's not one unmet promise after another but real accomplishment, little by little.

FAIR

A leader's fairness will most likely show up when he or she is alone with someone else, talking about a third party who isn't there. Will they represent the facts accurately? Will they provide an appropriate benefit of the doubt? Are they free from bias and dishonesty? Impartial and unprejudiced might be the best ways to describe a leader who is fair.

GRATEFUL

I've noted elsewhere that curiosity and gratefulness are high up on the list of characteristics I'm looking for in a leader. Gratefulness puts things in perspective because, first off, there's no false pride that something has really been earned. Grateful people understand that luck and circumstances are part of success, and they don't get too full of themselves.

HONEST

What sort of list would this be if we were describing a leader and didn't include honest? And how could you work well for someone you didn't trust and respect? It would be impossible. The last thing you need is a leader who says different things to different people, either because they're afraid of conflict or because they are trying to amass power.

HOPEFUL

Great leaders are hopeful, even when they know all the facts about the circumstances. That's not to say they're optimistic, which can mean that they're living in denial. Hopefulness is a founded belief in success. Follow the reasonable plan and find predictable results at the outset.

ACCEPTING OF A MINORITY POSITION

The group, however you define that, is often wrong. The supposed safety in numbers is elusive. In fact, nearly every moment of truth in the collective knowledge of a civilization has been characterized by a very small minority arguing their point until the masses climb aboard the idea.

This means that a leader will often look wrong to the majority of those that he or she manages, and they will have to be comfortable with that position in the minority.

Caution is called for, of course, because being in the minority doesn't mean you're right, either!

MERCIFUL FROM SIGNIFICANT PERSONAL FAILURE

Leaders are flawed, and they know it. They are plagued by some consistently surfacing weakness and/or some significant failure in the past. Maybe they've been fired, had personal financial difficulties, or were at the helm of a department that failed spectacularly. In any case, their personal failures haunt them to some extent, keeping them humble and merciful.

PATTERN MATCHER/CRITICAL THINKER

The essence of intelligence is the ability to notice and categorize patterns. Leaders have that critical thinking skill and use it to analyze business problems. They see the possibilities and the outcomes like few others do, and therefore can set an appropriate course of action.

PREDICTABLE

By suggesting that a leader needs to be predictable, I'm not meaning to imply negatively that they always act the same way regardless of the circumstances. No, it's more about those they lead being able to anticipate how a leader might think and or act.

PURPOSEFUL

A purposeful leader is one who does things with a purpose. They have a plan, can articulate it, and then see to it that the seemingly random activities of a typical day are actually contributing to the execution of the plan.

They aren't willy-nilly in all sorts of fits and starts. No, they see how the small parts contribute to the larger picture and they execute with that in mind.

SELF-AWARE

Good leaders are self-aware. They know their own tendencies, and they know how their actions affect others. They understand that their great strength, if overused, can be their greatest weakness, and they attempt greater balance and understanding. Good leaders can step outside themselves and make a relatively honest assessment of who they are and how they are conducting themselves.

STIMULATION PRIMARILY FROM OUTSIDE WORK

You'd think that any leader who throws himself entirely at work would be good to work for, but that's not the case. Leaders like that expect too much of others, too.

No, you want a leader who lives a more balanced life, understanding the role of work and the role of life outside work. A leader with an interesting life outside work is better at work/life balance issues.

VISIONARY

A leader must have a vision of the future. Otherwise, there's very little likelihood that individual initiatives will be purpose driven. Why does this department or firm exist? How could it be better? What role could we play in the larger picture that would bring greater enjoyment and impact?

FINALLY

How do you measure up against this list? Are there some things to work on? Do you see any patterns that hold you back? Make you very effective?

It's something to think about, anyway. As you'll see in a moment, great leaders instigate and nurture great culture. That connection is obvious, and so let's talk about culture next.

15

Creating and Sustaining Culture

You can't really talk about impactful culture without first talking about impactful leaders, but now that we've done that we can talk about culture.

What is it? What defines culture in an organization? One thing we know for sure is that it's not strongly connected to the "vision," "mission," and "culture" signs hanging in the lobby. Heck, the most evil companies in history said all the right things, and they said them in engraved marble in the lobby! No, culture isn't what you say.

Culture is what you do. Period. Even bigger than that, culture is the sum total of all your actions. You know that very talented employee who is selfish and territorial? Keeping that employee around speaks to the real culture at your firm. It says that you value output pretty much regardless of what comes with it.

Think about staff for just a minute. You're regularly making decisions about who you hire, how you hire them, how you reward or promote them, and who is dismissed. Even your own personal approach to honesty sets a standard that informs culture. All together, these actions demonstrate what you value. In other words, they determine your values. It's not what you say that determines your values but what you actually value, as demonstrated by your actions.

CULTURE: INTERNAL POSITIONING

It's very common and easy to talk about external positioning: what makes your product or service unique in relation to your competitors. When I'm talking about that with my clients, I'd typically say that six things must be true of your positioning in the marketplace. Recently I've realized that all of them can be applied to your internal positioning, too, so let's take a look at each one of them. This is important because in many cases I think it's more difficult to find the right employees than the right clients. Even if that's not true, having the wrong employees is a lot more detrimental to a firm than having the wrong clients. Starting with culture, then, helps you attract and keep the right employees.

Let's look at the six things that should be true of your culture.

First, your culture should be differentiated. That is, it should be different from the culture of other firms. Not just to be different, but because employees need a compelling reason to work for you. And, there's a lot of competition for the best employees. They can write their own ticket, so to speak, and you really only want to be hiring people who have all sorts of opportunities for employment.

How do you know if it's differentiated? If you can write the prime elements of your culture on a piece of paper, hand it to the principal of another firm, and have them read it as if it were their own to embrace, it's not differentiated. I suppose it goes without saying that you can't use someone else's thoughts when developing your own culture, because that's their culture, not yours.

Second, your culture should be demonstrable. By that I mean that a curious, intelligent stranger should be able to walk a single circuit through your facility and get a sense of your culture. There might not be any obvious clues (like a huge poster with a lifeless culture plastered on it), but there will be all sorts of smaller clues. Things like the tenor of conversational tone, the engagement of people talking to each other, the personal freedom of expression in each cubicle, and so on.

All that to say this: unless someone on the outside (who is curious and intelligent) can discern your culture, it's not demonstrable...which means it's not real.

Third, your culture should be sustainable. I don't mean sustainable in the ecological sense, but rather over time. Take a very customer-centric culture, for instance. Can any given employee continue to jump that high for decades, or will the process just wear them out to the point where they'll need to move on?

It's all about taking the long view. Can we maintain this indefinitely, or should we look at making some changes to render our culture more sustainable over time?

Fourth, your culture should be true. Obviously, your real culture is always true—by definition it must be. But if there's any dissonance between your stated culture and your real culture, employees will no longer care. They might even become cynical and mistrusting of the organization as a whole.

The constant barrage of advertising messages has yielded employees with finely tuned senses regarding inauthenticity. Be anything but authentic at your own peril indeed.

Fifth, your culture should be ethical. I suppose that goes without saying, but I really do need to say it anyway. But you know what that means and no further explanation is necessary. Is your culture ethical?

Sixth, your culture should be articulated. Every employee is not as curious or intelligent as the others in the group, and they'll need some explanation of what culture you're striving for. Besides, having a cultural vision in writing holds you more accountable from below. They'll notice gaps or deltas in the statement and the practice. That'll keep you on your toes, and that's a good thing.

So what do you do with an internal positioning for which these six things are true? Well, you'll do the same thing you'd do with a similarly effective external positioning. You'll develop a marketing plan!

That's right, a marketing plan. Remember what I noted above: good employees are harder to find than good clients, and that makes it worth looking hard for them. Nothing will change your management experience like the impact of having great employees.

HOW CULTURE IS CREATED

I noted above that culture is the sum total of your actions. More specifically, culture is created by three things. Let me enumerate and comment on each of these to help bring this discussion to bear on your situation.

First culture is created by the types of leaders you have in place. I don't mean just official leaders, either. Some of the most effective leaders in an organization are leaders only because they have followers. And they have followers because they are worth following. They're inspirational and other-centric.

This is naturally a good place to start because your chances of influencing a larger group of people are greater if the job can be shared with other leaders. At most you should have a half dozen or so people answering to you, so that leaves a large group of potentially untouched people that could easily be influenced if more (of the right type of) leaders were available to do just that.

Second, culture is created by the types of employees you have on staff. This may not seem different from that last point, but it is. You could have the right leaders and the wrong people and things would not be good. They'd be bad. You can assume that a good leader can improve an employee, but they have to have something to work with or it's so much wasted effort.

Third, culture is created by the management policies at your firm. Or lack thereof, I suppose. What do you say you want? This might be the actual words you use, spoken or written, or it might just be how your actions speak and what they demand or how people emulate them.

The common theme in these three elements of culture is choice. People making choices. People evaluating situations and deciding what to do or how to react.

Culture is the sum total of all your choices.

ENEMIES OF CULTURE

Despite your best efforts, though, there will be times when the culture you want will seem just out of reach. No matter how well you articulate the desired culture and make the right choices it still eludes you. What might cause that? The enemies of culture is our next topic.

The first enemy of culture is the technically proficient or very capable jerk. Deep inside you know that this individual doesn't represent the sort of employee you want, and that's true in every way —except their actual work. But you put up with the mismatch in culture because of some other reason: they are

157

technically proficient, have leveraged relationships with clients, or they just produce a lot. But putting up with something is nothing else but simply a compromise.

The second enemy of culture is not managing. The right employees might be in place, and even the right managers, but they're stuck doing things instead of managing things. We've talked about this extensively already.

The third enemy of culture is growing too quickly, which is usually accompanied by neglect of that middle layer of management. That inordinate rate of growth might be organic: the company is doing a lot of things well and the marketplace is acknowledging that. Or it might be via acquisition, requiring you to integrate two cultures.

The fourth enemy of culture is related to place, or your physical working arrangements. Culture by definition is a face to face activity, or at least the bedrock of culture is. So having employees work remotely (telecommuting from home) too much doesn't allow a culture to form. It's fragile and misunderstood.

Similarly, having people too crammed into a space that's too small provides what I call an emotional crowding that's difficult to overcome.

Even having people segregated by function and working on different floors can, in some circumstances, create fissures in a culture.

The fifth enemy of culture is not having enough work for people to do. When people have idle time on their hands, they do two things. They find things to whine about and they (rightfully) wonder why their leaders are allowing this to continue, either by not adjusting capacity downward or adjusting opportunity upward.

The sixth enemy of culture is having too much work for people to do. It feels good to be busy in the short run, but it can be demoralizing over time. It doesn't balance the amount of relaxation, introspection, and organization that forms a substantial part of the typical life of a firm.

The seventh enemy of culture is leadership disputes. This happens when partners or even key leaders are not on the same page. Even if they don't drop hints about each other's role in the dispute, the culture becomes territorial and self-serving.

The eighth enemy of culture is being client driven instead of client focused. No matter how you justify it, having an abusive client can tear at the fabric of a culture. Even having clients with too much control over the environment can be destructive, rendering a culture that's too reactive. You'll spend an inordinate amount of time just fighting back the jungle (clients with too much control) so that you can live in the campsite (your firm).

That's it. If everything seems pretty good but the right culture is still elusive, consider whether one or more of these is hindering your good efforts.

And don't forget to pay attention to the little things, either. Smile some more. Take the time to talk to an employee in the lunch room when you have a minute. Hand write a note of thanks. Send something to an employee's home, to be waiting for them when they get off work. Buy flowers for everybody one day.

Do whatever you want, really. The point is action, particularly if it's action that supports the culture you want to have. Do you want to nurture innovation? Then celebrate the occasional failure, because you can't have one without the other, right?

And by all means remember that culture is fluid and that it must change over time. Don't create culture and then become primarily the protector of culture. You might find yourself protecting outdated conventions that really should be changed anyway.

FINALLY

The uniqueness of your culture is either intentional or it is built in such a way as to adjust for your own dysfunction. It's your job to determine where the culture is on that continuum.

You might even select an archivist or historian of culture so that the culture is memorialized. If nothing else, doing so highlights its importance.

Remember this: great culture attracts great people and it spits out people who, in the end, don't match. It's polarizing, and that's a good thing.

Let's look next at the different styles of individual leaders and how that might come into play in impacting a culture.

16

The Different
Ways of Managing

When you're attempting to establish and then constantly impact a culture, your own natural style of interaction will certainly come into play. Are you energized when you rub shoulders with people, or are you more of an introvert, choosing different methods of influence? Even a small difference in how you interact will make a big difference in the methods you choose.

All of us have behavioral tendencies, like what makes us angry, how much freedom we need versus how much structure we crave, etc. Those behavioral tendencies, when taken as a whole, affect the extent and nature of your collaboration with others.

You may be impatient by nature, for instance. Couple that with an employee you manage that might need lots of direction, and suddenly you have a recipe for frustration. For both of you! You want to set a goal and have them find their own way toward it. They, however, would prefer that you outline the steps along that path so they can follow them and please you. You both want the same end result, but the method of getting there is quite different.

SUCCESSFUL PEOPLE

These examples merely illustrate the differences in innate behavioral style, whatever that is for you. And assuming that you want to be a successful person, key to that process will be understanding yourself, first, and then understanding how your behavior affects others. What makes you effective? What hinders your effectiveness? What sets you off? What are your preferred methods of working? I'd recommend that you take a personality profile or assessment, and read the results carefully. It's not as if you can't "step outside yourself" from time to time, but it will require more energy on your part, and it won't be a natural reaction to your circumstances.

What will you do with all the information that a typical personality profile might yield? For one thing, you'll want to align your own role with your natural strengths. If you are consistently required to do things that don't align with those strengths, you'll dread them, put them off, or just not be engaged in their accomplishment. We'll always have things to do that aren't our favorites, but if we can align most of our required behavior with our natural styles, we're more likely to be successful. If you require frequent mental stimulation and are easily bored, then it wouldn't make sense to align your tasks in a repetitive manner, right? It's all about understanding yourself better and better as you mature, and finding roles that fit your natural style.

Successful people also have a positive attitude about who they are, naturally, and they understand that their natural style is a strength and not a weakness. They frequently wish they were different, but that wish is really more about wishing that they could avoid overusing their strength.

That's the thing, too. While your natural tendencies are best viewed as a strength, they might also—if overused—become a liability. Your tendency to listen carefully to all the input around you might slide into a tendency to never make a decision quickly enough. Or your ability to relate well to others may slide into a desire to be liked, hindering you from making some of the tough choices that will inevitably come with a particular management role.

So it's about knowing who you are, including your strengths and weaknesses, and it's about knowing how to adapt your natural tendencies when the situation calls for it. That's in part what makes people successful.

WHO YOU ARE

Who are you? We can read your DNA, obviously, but that won't give us much information regarding your personality. There is no tool that allows us to read your core personality directly. Instead, we have to rely on reading your responses—those responses that flow from your core personality. Your observable behavior points to an underlying set of natural tendencies, and that behavior is generally a very good indicator of who you are.

Your responses and surface traits are observable, situationally based, flexible, dynamic, and based on thoughts, beliefs, and underlying personality.

So please take a personality profile and pay careful attention to what it says about your natural tendencies.

WHO OTHERS ARE

If successful people understand who they are and how they naturally react in any given situation, they don't stop there but take the same knowledge and begin to understand who the people are that they manage. Understanding yourself is foundational, but it's ultimately selfish if it stops there. You can't expect everyone to adapt their behavior to your preferences. It's actually more realistic if you adapt your behavior, wherever possible, to their expectations.

If nothing else, surely you can see the value in interacting differently with the different employees you manage. Imagine how much more effective you could be as their manager if you understood their natural preferences and style.

Seeing the world this way and then acting on it will ensure far greater success and enjoyment on the job. If someone doesn't like surprises and struggles to think on their feet, well, then don't surprise them and don't expect them to contribute meaningfully in brainstorming sessions with off the cuff questions. If someone needs a lot of variety, don't give them protracted, involved projects to work on. And so on.

Understanding your management style, and then understanding how others want to be managed, can go a very long way toward creating an environment where people (the managers and the managed) flourish.

I would strongly urge you to take a fresh personality profile assessment tool and then ponder it very carefully. It will be invaluable in your everyday management experience, and it will help you handle the transitions you're going to need to navigate as your management experience unfolds.

Let's look at those transitions next.

17

Required Transitions
To Be Effective

As your management experience unfolds, there will be very significant transitions to navigate. Encountering them doesn't indicate you're doing something wrong or that the planets have aligned in a way just to punish you—it simply means your management experience is normal.

In fact, there will be times when as a manager you'll feel out of control, exhilarated, lonely, overwhelmed, and even searching for new significance. Not only are these feelings normal, I'd go beyond that to point out that if it does not feel that way from time to time, you probably aren't taking the management experience seriously enough or are in some form of denial.

When these feelings surface, you'll have an opportunity to choose. You can choose to react appropriately or you can make the situation worse by reacting based on your feelings. That latter choice will feel natural and appropriate at the time, but it will be the wrong reaction.

Let me detail a few wrong reactions so you can look out for them and maybe head them off at the pass.

WRONG REACTIONS

The first wrong reaction to difficulties you'll experience is to go into a high control mode and seek to eliminate the messiness of the management environment. That might manifest itself in coming down hard on people, drawing artificial lines in the sand, insisting on rule keeping all out of proportion to the circumstances, etc.

Essentially you quit trusting people and try to control them. The problem is that you can't really control what they're thinking—instead, you take a stab at merely controlling their behavior, but their attitude is actually worse. And of course that's the root of the issue.

This instinct to control things is your perceived antidote to feeling out of control. You think people aren't listening to you or aren't respecting your directives, so you clamp down even harder, hoping to force compliance.

If the issue really is an obstinate employee who needs to be dismissed, well, then deal with the issue directly and dismiss them. It's not very productive to penalize the entire group just because you're deeply annoyed with a few people who, you fear, are infecting the others.

If you feel like things are spinning out of control, that's usually a sign that something else—something deeper—is amiss. Take a deep breath and look underneath the surface to see what's really happening.

The second wrong reaction to difficulties you'll experience is to go back into the craft or the technical expertise from which you were promoted. This tendency to retreat to an area of greater comfort is driven by the need to resolve some of the angst that comes from the less comfortable areas. In moments of panic or stress, you will always revert to an earlier stage in your life when you were more comfortable. Or at least where you were more used to the situation.

You already know this, but you need to be a leader. When you have your head down doing things that other people could do, every minute spent there is time that could be used more effectively if you were leading your people. Who, by the way, are really looking to you for leadership and not technical expertise.

Hiding behind a comfortable place won't solve anything. It just puts off the inevitable, and makes it even tougher to face once you get around to it.

The third wrong reaction to difficulties you'll experience is to make friends with employees. That seems like an odd thing to say, but real management duty puts tough situations on your plate. When you deal with them, you can upset people—just for doing your job. When it's difficult for you to deal with rejection or tension, it's not all that unnatural to want to befriend your employees, hoping that they'll simply comply because of the friendship.

The problem with befriending employees is that you can't do it evenly, and so some are left out of that inner circle. These outsiders, as they think of themselves, feel slighted and mistreated. And that's probably close to the truth.

The solution is to have kind and civil relationships with those that work for you, but to find your best friends at a peer level in the workplace or outside of work entirely. Friendship confuses management relationships and it's not a healthy thing.

The fourth wrong reaction to difficulties you'll experience is to "pull" on people for loyalty purposes. This tendency often manifests itself in strong hints about loyalty, which is defined as staying late, reporting on dissent, and other manipulative activities that shouldn't be necessary. It's a cultic reaction intended to force people to take sides. It even extends to individual interviews with employees, finding out if they are for or against the current management (regime).

Don't do it. Any loyalty you create will be artificial, and in the process of creating it you'll polarize the group of people answering to you.

GOOD TRANSITIONS

What transitions are useful, though, and even expected? Let's look at a few that you'll almost certainly encounter and help you see what might be on the other side that will make your life easier.

The first good transition to make is to begin hiring people for their expertise rather than for what they cost you. In the early days, you have a budget and you hire accordingly. You aim for whatever you can get for that price, and that's the best you can do. There simply isn't any more money, and expertise takes a back seat to available funds.

Eventually, though, you determine that expertise is more important than money. So you outline what you're looking for in great detail and you don't settle for less. You have a budget in mind, but the budget takes a back seat to the requirements for expertise. That means you may bust the budget. But in this scenario, one very qualified person may actually be equally as effective as two less qualified individuals.

The second good transition to make is to move from judging to shaping the work underneath you. I use those words advisedly. Judging is making decisions about the extent to which any given effort meets your own criteria. On one level it makes sense to monitor things in that way, but very little teaching takes place in that environment. And you're stuck inevitably in the loop over time.

It's better to shape the efforts underneath you, asking questions about why it was done that way and using every opportunity to teach that individual something that will make them more likely to do better work next time.

The third good transition to make is to understand that managing is a gray world (not black and white), and that managing is never finished. It's like mowing the lawn. As soon as you're done with one pass, it starts growing again and will eventually need to be "managed" yet again.

If you need a sense of finality in your work, you'll be sorely disappointed. You can very seldom check something off and never revisit it. The problems recur and require constant attention.

Speaking of which, the fourth good transition to make is to quit solving the same problems every day. If you find yourself in that situation, it's a sure sign you're not hiring well, not training well, or you're keeping yourself in the loop to an unhealthy extent.

If a single problem keeps cropping up every day, then it's probably the case that multiple problems keep surfacing every day. So try this: try to solve one of them in a way that's more permanent. It requires a little more time to do so, but you'll end up just one step further ahead tomorrow than you were today.

Just so you know, too, the method of solving problems in this way often involves more process, or at least looking at how work unfolds.

The fifth good transition to make is to really know who you are. To be aware of that inner core that doesn't require validation from those you are managing. That outlook with the courage to do the right thing regardless of the reaction others have, or even the consequences of your decision. We'll talk more about that shortly.

Anyway, just remember that being entrusted with management and leadership doesn't mean things will get neater. They'll actually get messier, with all sorts of transitions to navigate. Every time you think you have something figured out, the rules of the game change and there's something else to learn or solve. That's why management positions bring constant challenge.

18

Special Message
For You Control Freaks

There's not a lot to say on this subject, but management does seem to attract control freaks in inordinate numbers. My own experience as a control freak was a bit hilarious. I decided that it was time to research OCD (obsessive compulsive disorder) tendencies, and so I went online and ordered three books. Right. Not one book, but three. As I explained this to someone, she just laughed, nearly rolling around on the floor. Ordering three books on obsessive compulsive tendencies seems to confirm the diagnosis before even cracking one of the books, no?

Laugh along with me about that, but being a control freak is not pleasant. For the perpetrator or the victims. We don't need to get bogged down on this particular subject, but there are a few observations I'd like to make. I'll try to make them as kindly but directly as I can.

QUALITY VS. CONTROL

One common line of reasoning I frequently hear from control freaks is that they are fixated on quality and unless they act like a control freak, too many things slip through the cracks. It's as if no one quite measures up to their own standards, and so they're trapped inevitably in the loop of approvals, sign-offs, corrections, and always touching things at every step. It's no surprise, then, when they become a bottleneck and get even more frustrated.

This idea that the control freak acts in this manner to preserve quality is really just a ruse, however. Because if they were really that interested in quality, they'd put more systems and processes in place to ensure better quality. No, what's really happening is that they want control, and so they define the standard as how they would do it, and that can change on a whim.

If you're really concerned about quality, put the right systems and processes into place, along with the right people, and manage that way. Otherwise you'll be a bottleneck, and that is frustrating for you and frustrating for them.

In the bigger scheme of things, your standards probably aren't that important anyway. Frankly, you probably have people noodling the life out of projects, perfecting areas where no one notices except you.

THE TERRORS OF DELEGATION

Take that bottleneck illustration above: the insistence on seeing everything before it's approved. What's really at stake, here? To answer that question, I want you to picture something with me.

Assume that you're leaving on vacation tomorrow. Given that, what do you think you'd be doing today? We know the answer to that: you'd be putting everything you can in writing for one purpose, and that's to ensure that people wouldn't need to bother you on vacation. As a control freak, you're probably so inundated with detail while you are at work, that you really need a break when that vacation rolls around.

So you go on vacation and sure enough, all those notes explaining things worked. No one had to bother you and things went pretty darned well, right? They didn't need you like they normally do.

But the story doesn't end there, right? You get back to work and everything goes back to the way it was before. A little bit of chaos. A lot of scurrying around. You touching everything like before, ensuring that things are done well.

Stop for a second and think about this, though. You put everything in writing so that you wouldn't be bothered. So it stands to reason that you don't put things in writing because you do want to be bothered! What other explanation could there be?

This explains some of your control freak tendencies and your reticence to put better systems and processes in place: it's designed so that you are kept inevitably in the loop.

PRESERVING YOUR MENTAL HEALTH

I'll end this very brief chapter by making some suggestions that might help keep your control freak tendencies in check.

First, recognize that these tendencies will always be there. You can learn to see them coming, work at taming them, and even avoid them at some points, but you won't be able to eliminate them.

Second, recognize that your greatest weakness is actually your greatest strength. It's just a matter of degree and focus. Don't overuse it or that strength becomes a weakness.

Third, recognize that you will always be misunderstood to some degree. That just comes with the territory. This could feed your tendency to be even more of a control freak, but you must not let that happen.

Fourth, keep your paranoia to a dull roar. The world is not out to get you, and your fears simply make you see things behind the shadows.

Finally, know who you are, keep a careful eye on what's important to you in the management environment, and then just don't worry about the rest of the mess. Your job is to do what the business needs, and to take care of the people.

Speaking of that, let's talk about how you might manage a bit more openly than usually expected.

19

Managing More Openly

The concepts behind open book management have been around for quite some time, but as an identified management discipline it's only been with us for a few decades. It's often abbreviated as OBM. There are some elements of the OBM movement that are worth incorporating into your management practices. If you feel like you need to get the basics down first, just skip this chapter for now and come back to it later.

OBM is not just opening your financial statements, though that misconception would be common. It's about much more than that, which is partly what makes this topic so appealing. First, it covers sharing financial information, obviously. Most of this information is on financial statements, but much of it is not. For example, you might talk about utilization, the cost of mistakes, or the profitability of certain client segments. This ancillary data is based on financial statements, but OBM goes further than the statements themselves by explaining what the data means and how individual activity affects it.

OBM also involves giving some decision making authority to those whose performance drives the numbers. In other words, OBM is not just "opening the financial books" but "managing openly" so that it's less of a top-to-bottom arrangement. OBM also involves some degree of tying rewards to company, group, and individual performance. This makes more sense in an OBM environment because people understand where the company is and how their individual actions affect that position. You can see this in a crude way: if a sales person is compensated on new business, they want to see an accounting of all the new business they have brought in, and they want to have some input in the marketing plan.

We shouldn't use information to intimidate, control, or manipulate people, though unfortunately this happens quite frequently. We should instead teach them how to work together to achieve common goals and thereby gain control over their lives. At least to whatever extent that is possible. They might do everything perfectly and still get laid off, but at least it won't come as a surprise if they are operating within an OBM environment!

Nevertheless OBM is largely financial. There's no way around this, either. Whether you are comfortable with it or not, numbers are still the language of business and the currency of success. (If you make lots of money, you won't necessarily be happy. Good business people don't just make money—they make money without giving up happiness.)

Frankly, I would welcome a return to more emphasis on numbers in our management practices. With a few exceptions, there is too much "rah rah" and too little emphasis on numbers. It's okay to do white water rafting for a weekend, climb simulated mountains on a local wall, bring a yoga instructor into your office, or sponsor Friday afternoon beer parties, but you can't forget one thing. You can't forget to make money to stay in business. Emotions have a legitimate role, but not at the expense of numbers, which are less likely to lie to you.

It's not about whether you use OBM or not, either, but rather to what degree you use it. We are all on a continuum. At one end we might only disclose that we are "having a good (or bad) month." Further along we might talk about specific sales numbers. At the end of the spectrum everyone will see the financials and be privy to compensation arrangements.

This just demonstrates that we all draw the line in different places. Personally I cannot recommend that you publish compensation data. When employees know what others make (except for direct managers), it usually means we have a bad morale problem that has led to this comparison. It also means that nothing good can come of it, if only because we cannot easily separate assigning work value and personal value.

Stepping back and looking at the landscape, it's clear that companies are doing better. They are providing better quality and better service, all within better cost structures. Competition and technology are powerful shaping forces.

But people aren't doing as well. They are sometimes anxious and frustrated. They are viewing employers with increasing mistrust and misgiving. They are cynical, and their icon is Dilbert. Something must be wrong, so let's move to the theory behind OBM and see if you buy it.

Access to information is control. Control allows change. Change allows contentment, only because we all want impact.

As you may have found, corporate reorganizations or deep work with a management consultant are self-limiting because they do not take place from the bottom up. Management consultants work from outside, and reorganizations take place from above.

You (as in "you" the manager) can only accomplish so much because there is only so much you can control. Ultimately, I suppose you could fire everybody, but there is a certain diminishing payout with that approach. Once you've got your systems humming again, your mistakes low, and your quality high, there's just not much left to fix in a lasting way. And of course your better competitors have already done pretty much the same things that you have, to a greater or lesser degree.

Your performance may be as good as theirs, but it's not likely to be measurably better. From this point forward there are only a few things left to boost performance over the long term, and one of those things is to have employees work enthusiastically and effectively and to take responsibility for their own work. Good procedures are indispensable. But what makes the difference in the end is whether the employees doing the job think about doing it just a little better and even care about whether they do or don't do it better.

Having said this, somebody still needs to lead, and your employees are probably not entrepreneurial leaders or they wouldn't be working for you. So let's not fool ourselves and go too far. "Animal Farm" doesn't even work in a book.

But if you do want that edge, it just might be openness in your management environment. While this might not be true in the strictest sense, openness is ownership and I can promise you've muttered the refrain: "I just wish they would think like owners."

Openness really is ownership because we are talking about ownership of information, ownership of responsibility, and ownership of results. An open environment provides all participants with an understanding of the intent of their organization. And it also provides them with the capacity to comply with that intent, if they wish, and then be accountable.

After all, when you understand, agree with, and have the capacity to comply, it's pretty hard to hang around and not embrace the organization's intent.

There are many advantages to a more open approach to management. The specific ones will vary based on your circumstances, but these three will probably be universal.

First, employees will take less for granted. Most people don't understand that 45% (or more) of gross profit goes to salaries and that up to 40% of net goes to taxes (depending on your structure and compensation methods). Until they learn otherwise, they might very well assume you are making lots more money than you really are.

They also don't know things like what retained earnings are or how a company might be making money but still be cash poor temporarily. They don't necessarily appreciate how a mistake comes straight out of profit and how thin margins really are. Did you understand that stuff before you owned your own company or became an important manager? Did you ever complain about things, "unhindered by data"?

Second, there will be fewer unfounded rumors. In the absence of real facts, people tend to fill the void with rumors about all kinds of things. You can set the record straight easily and let employees concentrate on other things, like not filling out their timesheets.

Third, employees will have a larger perspective. As you talk through the numbers and your plans to deal with them, people will begin to see the connection between their activities and the bottom line. You will also give them a sense of ownership because they understand and have impact.

All this teaches them that to be a viable company you need profit. Your survival and comfort depend on it. Sure, people are frequently told what to do in an eight hour day, but they aren't shown how that activity fits into the bigger picture. For example, when is the last time you walked through the time bid on a particular project and placed that against the time actually spent?

With these obvious advantages, why is implementing OBM so difficult to do? I've noted three reasons in working with various entrepreneurs.

First, entrepreneurs don't let go. They are control freaks, and as long as they control information they can control the decisions.

Second, entrepreneurs crave independence. They don't want to "build consensus" and stop for obstacles. It's easier to filter the data and ask people to take statements at face value rather than pause to give people a chance to digest and then approve. And what if they don't approve? Entrepreneurs would rather ask forgiveness than permission.

Third, it only looks more difficult in a small company. The only big companies that disclose financials are the publicly held ones, and that only because they are required to do so by the SEC. Of course they are generally run by non-entrepreneurs, which makes it even easier to comply.

If you go ahead with it, though, you'll need to be prepared.

First, you must be excited about this. If another party, whether a group of managers or a group of employees, is pushing you toward this, it will fail. You can still be skeptical but you have to believe it's the right thing to do. If there are others with you in the management group, there should be a clear consensus to do it.

Second, you can't do this just by department—it must be for the whole company. One of the most frequent disputes is over how to allocate overhead expenses, and there will be too many disagreements about who should be charged with the conference room, the copy machine, and the new server. Any open book system smaller than an entire company will only work in very large companies with very clear divisions.

Third, you need to make sure that your company is ready for the increased scrutiny and that there is as little room as possible for confusion. To do this, make sure you are receiving regular, accurate financials. Those financials should reflect only company transactions, too. In other words, don't intertwine your personal life. Get those personal cars and loans and expenses off the corporate books.

You'll also want to spend some extra time making sure your managers understand the new data at least as well as the employees do—hopefully better.

And finally, make sure that the financial data you will be talking through is forward looking. In other words, include not just historical data, but also budgets, cashflow projections, and something about your planning process.

All this to say that you should think carefully about why you are doing it. List the reasons for yourself, then ask yourself which ones are part of a larger philosophical picture versus a more momentary need.

In other words, this is much easier to do when things are bad and you need everybody's help. But how will you feel when things are good and the disparity between your compensation and theirs had widened again?

Speaking of this, there is one very dangerous reason to implement OBM, and it is based on the belief that more information will create a "self-managed environment." This is precisely where OBM fails because it expects results from a management system that can only come from managers (vs. systems). In other words, OBM is a system which helps managers do a better job, not a system which lessens the need for management.

So let's agree that we aren't trying to turn our people into rats who will run the maze with a smile on their faces. Nor are we trying to avoid the inevitable grayness otherwise called management. Instead, we are trying to do the right thing, looking for ways to clarify our expectations of people and to say thank you when they meet them. We are also trying to give them the tools to take more personal control of their environment. But

OBM will not necessarily remove some of the need to manage people.

The place to start is with an environment that complements the system instead of nullifying any benefits it might bring.

This is important because unless there is a good environment employees won't believe the numbers, and unless they believe the numbers this won't work. There is no amount of disclosure that will reassure a skeptical employee if only because all of the reports are self-generated.

This skepticism is not unfounded in companies with difficult management environments. For too long numbers have been used to punish, supervise, intimidate, and control. In this case, though, we are talking about education. To be more specific about what it means to create an effective environment, here are three specific suggestions.

First, assess your company. Look it over from top to bottom, assessing how effectively your company is poised to embark on some change. Do this yourself or hire an outsider to take a look.

How's the morale? What would you change about your company? What would employees change? If you have to guess at their answer to this last question, why is it that employees fear being forthright with you?

How's the infrastructure? Do people know who their single supervisor is? Is that supervisor really managing people, or just providing technical advice on how to do things? Do you see accurate, timely numbers? Do you understand them and believe them yourself?

If I want to quickly assess the morale in a company, I typically just ask about it in a confidential employee survey, and usually employees are honest about it. But the best way to get at that information through the back door is to ask how conflicts are handled. Poorly managed environments sweep conflicts under the rug, or they are handled in a manner that is not appropriate (too publicly, through the wrong medium, etc.).

Second, have you gone through some big changes recently? These might include the loss of a key employee under less than stellar circumstances. Or a move into new facilities that required far longer than you would have liked. Or very poor results that fall far outside the norm. Or a divisive employee retreat. Or a controversial new personnel policy.

In general, OBM is best implemented from a stable platform. Not only will your motives be clear, but employees will not be distracted.

Third, how good a job has your company done in the past at adapting to change? Sure, OBM requires more change on your part than on theirs, but there is some adapting that needs to come from all quarters. I would draw your attention to one very significant point: by definition an entrepreneur's tolerance for change is far greater than the tolerance of an average employee. Employees generally value stability. You probably place a higher value on change and challenge. Step into their shoes and try to view change on a grand scale from their perspective.

Working through these three questions will help you predict the success of a more open environment. Where is your company right now? What major events have you faced recently? How well do your employees adapt to change? The main point is that you must be willing to address the larger context in order to give OBM a fighting chance to succeed.

If you're with me so far and want to try this, start small and work your way up.

First, decide who will be involved. The choices are obvious: owners, key managers, project managers, employees, clients, and competitors. This answers the question of "who" will be involved.

Unbelievably, many owners—especially the ones who participate less in managing the internal business affairs—know very little about what goes on. This is unconscionable, and it's the place to start for a more open environment. After all, employees are likely to ask any owner questions about what the data means, and any owner should be able to answer those basic questions.

Key managers are those who regularly participate in steering the firm. They are consulted on areas outside their immediate influence, contributing to discussions about employee culture, facility usage, marketing initiatives, and customer service standards, to name a few.

Project managers are those who track details or provide technical expertise to lesser experienced employees. They shape projects more than people. They function more like senior employees than managers.

Employees are comprised of the rest of the crew, though you might also want to include full-time freelancers who for all practical purposes function as employees.

Competitors are those other firms who hire your employees and pump them for information, or who read the information you release to the press (e.g., on your sales revenue).

Second, decide what information you will divulge. While you could obviously divulge all of it, few firms do. Instead, they pick and choose elements that are appropriate for their situation. As such, you need to develop your very own dashboard.

The dashboard in your car is not designed for you specifically. If it were, the gauges that mean the most to you would be positioned front and center, and their relative size would complement their relative importance. In much the same way, consider designing your own financial dashboard. The key is to choose meaningful metrics and then explain them carefully to employees.

What are these critical numbers? The answer depends on where you are and what you are struggling with (which suggests that they will change over time). These are the movements in your firm that are preventing you from being success-ful or helping you keep the success that you enjoy. And they can almost always be measured in financial terms.

But of course these should be part of a larger plan so that you don't fixate on them. And what is that plan, by the way? The specific data you want to watch has everything to do with the specific goals you want to achieve. If you are not interested in getting bigger, don't talk all the time about gross revenue; instead, concentrate on net profit.

Not only should you be strategic in your measurements (concentrating on what you want to see different), but you should also be dynamic (watch it regularly) and holistic (what other plans will we need because of these efforts?).

After you've decided what to measure, set a benchmark or a goal for each number. You might even want to establish a time frame within which you'd like to meet the goal.

Next, identify the operations that affect this measurement. These are performance drivers. To illustrate, if we want a higher net profit, we'll need a combination of these things: higher esti-mates, fewer expenses, fewer mistakes, less wasted time, etc. To achieve a greater cash cushion, we'll need to take more cash in than we expend without incurring long term obligations. That means greater profitability and harder work.

Then after listing all the possible factors that might affect the outcome you desire, identify the best current opportunities and weaknesses that could be exploited. These will be the first places to concentrate as you chase the goal.

Next, track these metrics regularly. Report to the interested parties with a simple cover summary, backed up by lots of detail for those who are interested. Educate in the reporting, because financials will not be useful unless they are understandable, timely, unbundled (by department, if that applies to your situa-tion), and with an element of forward looking.

Meetings are generally the best places to disseminate this information because they allow you to capture reactions and answer questions in real time. But also use bulletin boards, big charts that make a single point, intranets, handouts, newsletters, and emails. You are always anticipating questions. What does this mean? How will my actions affect the bottom line?

As you open the books, so to speak, tell them the stories behind the numbers. Let the data serve as a discussion point about what you really want to talk about.

Finally, after things have settled down and people begin to learn this new language of OBM, consider tying some compensation to financial metrics.

Whatever the extent to which you implement OBM, make sure you begin the orientation to that system at the hiring stage. In other words, tell people that "we do this here," showing them what types of information they'll be privy to and how it might be interpreted.

If they are hired, provide extensive training during the orientation process. Of course include a statement about non-disclosure in your employee agreements.

If you want to take it a step further, you'll find that OBM works best if these things are true at your firm.

First, everyone should understand what the company must do to be successful.

Second, make sure everyone is involved in the goal setting process. This will help with the next point.

Third, everyone should understand their individual role in achieving the goals that define "success."

Fourth, problem solving and decision making should be done at a level closest to the issues to be solved. This assumes, of course, that the employees have the bigger picture.

The point is that OBM is not an "on" or "off" proposition. It's just a greater degree of openness. There are several things you'll want to keep in mind, particularly if you think OBM will solve everything. There are three things I'd urge you not to assume.

First, don't assume that people will act smarter with information. Even trade groups can't show more than a few percentage point gain in profitability when employees know the numbers.

Second, don't assume that every employee will be fair. Some people will misuse the information and you must be prepared for that.

Third, don't assume that people will not measure each other's value with financial criteria, whether that's compensation data (which you shouldn't divulge) or sales or client conversion or whatever else can be expressed in numbers.

Best wishes on your critical quest for a more satisfying management experience, for you and others.

One method of keeping it satisfying for you is to come to a comfortable work/life balance. Let's look at that next. But get ready—I'm going to get on my soapbox.

20
Maintaining Work/ Life Balance

I have had the privilege of working with hundreds of professional service firms over the years, spending at least one full day and countless hours with each principal, and also interacting with thousands of the employees who make things happen at these firms. I say "privilege" because it's stimulating to be around their energy, creativity, independence, humor, and "otherness." I love my work.

Because I've been successful in that work, many people informally ask me questions about starting businesses, fixing businesses, and even buying/selling businesses. This might happen over a drink or a meal. One of the concepts that frequently surfaces is this idea that people ought to pursue what they love and success will follow. "Just follow your passion and the success will take care of itself."

Bullshit. There are a lot of people following their passion who are on the edge of starving. They've oriented a work life around themselves that meets their basic need for stimulation, and in the process they've made all sorts of compromises on the fundamental business issues.

This fallacy extends to management, too. "If it's not fun I shouldn't be doing it." That's nonsense, too. Management and leadership are very hard work indeed, and if it's high on your list to shun the things that aren't stimulating, you'll be ignoring some basic management and leadership duties that just plain aren't fun. But are necessary.

As I noted in an earlier chapter, I think you're looking for the wrong things from your job. Almost all of you are afflicted with S.D.D. (stimulation deficit disorder), compounded by a nearly constitutional belief that you have the right to find the cure in your work.

Thank goodness there aren't more people like you. We'd have no coffee because it's kind of boring to grow, truth be told. And I know, because I used to do it. I grew up in Costa Rica and Guatemala and understand what a subsistence culture is. You want some coffee? Grow it, assuming you have the land and climate. Need some sandals but don't really have a spare cow for the leather? Maybe grow some extra coffee and trade it to the guy who can't grow it...but does have cows and the time to make sandals.

Work was work and play was play. Actually, work still is work and play still is play for most of the world. Pharmacists at Wal-Mart got into the field because they wanted to help people, but there's not tons of excitement counting pills and having the same discussions with old men about their common ailments. Architects love building visible monuments and tackling design problems through the creative use of building materials, but most of their day is boring. I have a good friend who's a space shuttle astronaut and it's not nearly as glamorous as you'd think.

My point is that the world would be a very different place if every worker demanded a high level of creative stimulation. In your ideal world, it wouldn't matter that this design project has to meet specific business criteria or be finished by a certain date. Instead, you'd be like Mozart, supported in style so that you'd be free to create, free of the encumbrances we call practicality, usefulness, or even convention.

I can hear the screaming now: "But look at the music he created!" The difference is that he's an artist and you aren't. That's right, I said that you are not an artist. That's not your job. Your job is to employ an unbelievably valuable skill to business problems.

The work you do operates on certain principles. Within those conventions we should be as unique in our application as we can get away with and still solve a business problem, but no more (especially if the client isn't paying for it).

I'm not using any big words here, and each of you would nod your head and agree with this perspective of the role that business plays. But after you put this book back down, you'll be tempted to go right back to the endless chase for stimulation.

But is that bad? When I talk like this, most people stare at me like they don't understand why this is a big deal at all. After all, what could be wrong with a very stimulating job, especially if you get rich in the process? That's a good question, and I'm going to give you five reasons why I think it's dangerous to medicate your S.D.D. with your chosen profession.

First, expecting too much stimulation from your work will result in compromised business decisions. Compromised business decisions are usually subtle, but over time they yield a blunt instrument.

Second, expecting too much stimulation from your work will result in too much drama because you will be too close to the product or service. If everything you do contains even just a little bit of yourself, clients will find it difficult to interact with you about your work. They'll fear that you will take such discussions personally, when in fact all they want to do is speak about the business effects of your work.

Third, expecting too much stimulation from your work will result in disappointment with clients if their mission doesn't overlap with your personal one.

Fourth, expecting too much stimulation from your work will result in early burnout because you won't be running a sustainable business.

Fifth, expecting too much stimulation from your work will result in less of a life. Your focus is on the job. Long hours aren't a huge problem because "this is something I enjoy." Making a bit less money than you could otherwise make is okay because of the fun you are having. But both of these results (less time and less money) create an environment where you no longer have much of a life after work. You're tired, there's little time, and there may not even be the money you'd need to pursue that hobby.

Remember what you used to do for creative stimulation outside your current vocation? Maybe it was flying, photography, painting, travel, reading, or surfing. Whatever it was, you'd have a much healthier business and personal life if you separated the two. Together, there's too much overlap. Too much confusion. Too many compromises. Grow the coffee and use the extra money to buy the sandals.

Having said that, there is no future whatsoever in having a job that you don't enjoy. But demanding that your job be enjoyable, and then making decisions to protect that aspect of it, may very well backfire. Some times hard work that's just good, honest, grinding hard work is good for the soul. It teaches us discipline, appropriateness, and measured contribution. Oh, and best of all, it can fund a very fun personal life apart from work! Is it time for you to treat your business more like a business, and your personal life more like something you'd never trade for anything?

I'll get off my soapbox, now, but I wanted to plant some seeds about achieving balance in the work/life equation. Thanks.

21

Finally

So far we've covered quite a lot of ground in relation to your own management experience. Some of that has been necessary only because you had to start largely from scratch. You were dropped behind enemy lines, so to speak, and had to begin fending for yourself immediately.

Can you imagine how much better your initial management experience would have been if you'd been prepared? If someone had taken you under their wing and given you enough preparation to not only know what was coming but to actually teach you some basic principles of management ahead of time?

That's really what I'd like you to think about—how you can pave the way for future managers and have an impact on their experience in that transition from doing to managing. There's terrific potential for impact, here. So let me make four specific suggestions on how best to do that.

TWO CAREER PATHS

The first suggestion is to not put someone on a management path unless they're really a fit for it. As we discussed earlier, many managers get put on that path because they've climbed to the top of the craft path and the supervisor feels the need to have them make more money. They feel that the only way to justify this is if they take on management responsibility, which is something they aren't good at, and don't have an interest in.

So clearly identify two tracks and don't make managers out of technically competent experts unless there's strong evidence of management aptitude.

DELEGATE RESPONSIBILITY

The second suggestion is to find smaller things you can delegate. Put someone in charge of the intern program, or maybe of the employee intake process. Use special projects to identify and test management ability. Say, for example, that you have a problem with timekeeping compliance. Give the project to a promising young manager, who can determine the real problem, make some suggestions, build consensus, and follow through over time. You'll get a sense of their management style, but even more importantly, you'll have an opportunity to give them feedback on the process. It never hurts to help them build confidence, either.

SPEND EXTENDED TIME AWAY

The third suggestion is to find opportunities to spend extended time away. Spending a week away at a time would be normal, so spend two weeks away at a time. Put someone in charge and rotate that responsibility. Instead of calling you every day to give you an update, have them keep a log or diary of the key decisions and how they handled them. That narrative will produce all sorts of interesting talking points when you return.

MINIMIZE PROMOTIONS

The fourth suggestion is to minimize any promotions you give out. Remembering that real management and leadership has very little to do with official titles, you don't want to train your people that good effort is always rewarded with a new title or bump in pay.

We learn this nonsense back in kindergarten, from which kids actually graduate! How crazy is that. The last thing we need is to over-promote people simply because frequent promotions are expected. Instead, train people to realize that doing good work for the right reasons is enough of a reward, and that promotions are rare and exceptional things.

That's it. We've looked at a list of some simple things you can do to make the experience of the managers who follow you better than your own experience likely was. I think you'll find that it's very satisfying to help people in such substantive ways.

Let me wrap things up, now, with some final suggestions.

COLLECT THINGS

Being a pack rat isn't always good, but pretend that someone is going to do a documentary about you some day and they'll want some specific artifacts to weave into the story. Your job is to collect those things over the years.

The list might include the cork from a wine bottle from a meal at which you had a very significant conversation with someone that you manage. Or maybe some encouraging notes.

Maybe even a very critical note that felt like it would destroy you at the time but which now you look back on as formative in your management career.

Anyway, start collecting things that tell your story. Then, when you have a few moments every few months, look through what you've collected and enjoy the memories. At the moment I have 263 email messages in my "Unsolicited Praise" folder. Each of them mean a lot to me, and they help me get a better perspective when I'm discouraged...or I've messed up.

SCREW THE IMPLICATIONS

What an odd piece of advice, no? I really mean it, though. We're too slow to make the right decisions, agonizing over the implications of doing the right thing. There are times when you need to do the right thing even in spite of the dire implications that come from doing it.

Don't think too much about all this stuff, including this advice.

REMEMBER THAT THE TRUTH ALWAYS SURFACES

When you're misunderstood—which is going to happen a lot, by the way—you can't scurry around making sure everyone knows the real story. No, just do the right thing (see above) and let the truth surface on its own.

Someone is holding the truth down, of course, but they'll either get tired of doing that or it'll seep to the surface on its own. Just like holding an inner tube under water is exhausting, so too is holding the truth from view.

You will be vindicated. Maybe not today or tomorrow or even this year, but you will be vindicated at some point.

In the end, too, this cannot matter too much. (Don't you wish I'd told you that before you read this book?)

Just eat right, be physically active, maintain strong friendships outside work, take lots of time off, lead an interesting life, and always be ready to leave your position so that you'll have the power and influence before you actually have to leave.

Best wishes in your management experience.

Appendix:
Shared Experience
of New Managers

I asked dozens of new managers to answer this question: "What tips would you pass along to others in your shoes?" Here are some of the responses, quoted with permission.

§

Find a balance between knowing your potential along with your limitations so you can be comfortable saying 'no' when it's required. It's a process to find that balance but like everyone else says, do not be afraid to make mistakes and learn from them when you make them.

§

First, explain your perspective/opinion supported by sound decision making and logic. Second, keep project objectives in mind vs. personal objectives. Third, above all else: listen.

§

Weigh the manager responsibilities against what you enjoy doing and see if they match up before you take the position. I really enjoy management and I believe it is a better fit for me than doing, but if you cannot let go of the doing yourself and feel competitive with the people you are managing from a doing perspective, you will fail. You have to be in a position to find satisfaction in the success of the team you manage. If you constantly feel in competition, or you feel you need to create the final product yourself to feel complete, management is not for you.

§

You can't assume you will have any respect or favor with new employees just because of your title. Developing trust is a two-way street. If someone refuses, you shouldn't assume they'll get over it if you continue to show that you have their best interests in mind. They are already tainted against you for some reason or another and that isn't likely to change unless there is an intervention. If you know an employee is most likely lying and you've given them plenty of chances to fess-up, you probably need to talk it over with your supervisor—it's not a sign of your weakness or ineffectiveness—but a problem based on misunderstandings or ill-feelings and needs to be corrected ASAP.

§

Be patient and be as clear as you can. I remember my dad telling me a long time ago that great athletes generally tend to make poor coaches and managers because the path they took to achieve their success was much different than the average player they are coaching. It's harder to relate to people that have a harder time grasping things whether it's having the range and positioning to cover more centerfield or having a keen eye for laying out an annual report. That has stuck with me. I'm not saying I'm a superstar, but I do believe I have another level of talent that involves being both creative and understanding of how a company needs to operate from a business point of view.

§

I don't think our group takes managing people seriously. Meaning, they don't carve out chunks of time or resources dedicated to managing others. Workers at all levels are expected to manage projects, people, and do work all at once. I often feel like I spend all day coordinating projects and people, and then my "real work" begins at 4pm. My advice in this area would be to get clear with superiors about what they are asking of you—are you a manager or doer? How much of each? And make them empower you with the resources (time, knowledge, title) needed to do either or both.

§

Think of all the managers you've worked under. Most of them probably did something really well. If you can combine all those positive traits you will definitely be on the right path to being a successful manager. Also, always gripe up, never down.

§

Jumping from doer to manager is great when you feel you have a handle on how the business is run and that you can offer insight, coaching, and training to those with less experience. If you are not a people person or hate to deal with many, many questions and requests, this is not the job for you. Be ready for stressful situations. Be ready to deal with a myriad of requests, paperwork, and rules. You have to become an enforcer and mentor. You need to set boundaries, but know when you can break them. Treat the employees with equal respect and learn the strengths and weaknesses of each individual in the department. Make an effort to push each person to try new things as they can tend to get bored and burned out.

§

It is important to sound constructive when correcting or changing a person's approach or process. I found this sometimes very difficult to do in a non-judgmental way. As a superior one must absolutely restrict comments to the work/project at hand, and give logical, understandable reasons. Do not sound arbitrary. Sounding constructive when being constructive is many times harder than it sounds, especially when dealing with some of the more insecure workers. But it is imperative to keep the department professional and your leadership respected.

Do not try to treat all workers the same. They are not, in personality type, in aptitude level, or in client interaction. Some workers respond well to positive reinforcement; some get lazy. Some need to be constantly challenged. And your over achievers will resent it if they are treated the same as your more average performers. This can be a hard tightrope to walk, as you don't want to be viewed as playing favorites but it is not impossible. Most of the time your employees know who they are and where in the competence level they fall.

Also share as much information as you have with your staff. Transparency builds confidence, rapport and respect. Hoarding information breeds contempt and resentment.

Understand what it really is that you're getting into before accepting a management position—especially the politics of those who are managing from above. I'm not advising that someone get involved in the politics, just understand them and the motivations for them. It's also helpful to know in advance that when you're managing from the middle, it's difficult to gain support since either side of you is instead looking for your support of them.

§

Don't accept a management position.

§

Take time for team building off-site activities. We've taken a few hours to see an exhibition of a well-known industrial designer in a near-by city. We've gone to the city for an afternoon at the Arts Festival. We've made trips to galleries and museums. Often they have a relationship to our work because that's part of what we have in common but it isn't necessary. These outings have been pre-approved and supported by upper management.

§

First, acknowledge that a good worker doesn't automatically translate into a good manager. You may not be ready for the transition. (That acknowledgement is the first step in seeking help.) Then seek help. Do everything you can to surround yourself with good people who will help you grow.

Second, understand that things will need be different. Your lunch crowd might need to be different. The things you discuss at the water cooler will need to change. At the same time you don't want the new position/power to go to your head. Otherwise, no one on your team will respect you.

§

Find something you like about everyone you work with. And whenever you feel like you can't stand that person another second, think of the good qualities that person has. I can honestly say that I don't dislike anyone I work with. I wouldn't choose many of them to be friends had we met outside the workplace, but at least they have my respect. And I deserve the same from them. I don't require that anyone likes me, but they need to treat me with respect.

§

If you are interested in rising to a management position, try teaching part time. It will help you develop skills that are directly transferable to a supervisory role. I am also currently working on team building exercises I can work on with my department. Spending time with my colleagues outside of the office working on an activity with a creative focus may help boost their morale and stimulate their creativity.

§

Never get comfortable at work. Keep on learning. It's easier to transfer to other departments and its easier to become an asset to the company when knowledge keeps building up. Who knows what you'll end up doing next?

§

Listen to your instincts - my gut feeling has almost always been right.

Respect people and they'll respect you.

Allow people to do great things. Once I let go and allowed my people to express themselves and embrace a project completely, they usually surprise me in a very positive way. My job got easier and much more rewarding seeing the people around me succeed and get excited by their success. I always try to provide direction and leadership, but allow them to have real ownership in a project.

§

Try to stay as true to your passion as you can. I have always liked solving problems for business. So this profession has worked out for me. I have two sons and the other day we were talking about careers and what they wanted to be. They asked me what I would do if I didn't own this firm. I really thought about it and I could not think of another job I wanted.

§

Be comfortable with yourself, accept your role as a coach and a leader, and nurture your people.

§

Seriously consider how your job influences your identity and analyze what kind of fulfillment you expect from your job. Be real about your abilities (ask others to help you evaluate your strengths because you can fool yourself).

Understand that this is still a business.

Commit yourself to learning (attend seminars, seek advice from managers you respect, read books, hire a consultant, etc.).

§

Think about your bosses that sucked, and don't do what they did.

Always treat people with respect, even when you're trying to make your presence felt.

Make management fun. You may need to get creative to do this, but you won't last long if you don't enjoy it.

§

Be humble. When possible, be a working manager so you can identify with what the team is experiencing on a daily basis. Always come from a position of strength and be a relentless advocate for your team to upper management.

§

Don't let the power of management go to your head. Treat your direct reports exactly how you would want to be treated.

§

Don't let it go to your head and don't get paranoid.

ABOUT THE AUTHOR

To read about or contact the author, please see:

www.davidcbaker.com

ROCKBENCH PUBLISHING CORP.

RockBench is an independent publisher based in Nashville, TN, focused largely on traditionally printed books with the support of digital content and interactive media. We provide thought leaders a larger platform for their work with businesses.

FORTHCOMING TITLES

The Win Without Pitching Manifesto
  by Blair Enns

Financial Management of a Marketing Firm
  by David C. Baker

RFP—Rarely Functional Process: Why the RFP Selection Process Fails Buyers and Sellers
  by Cal Harrison

Monday-Friday: A Year's Worth of Weekday Advice
  by David C. Baker

CREDITS

Cover design by faceoutstudio, Bend, OR

Cover photo by the author.

Book design by the author.

Titling typeface: Myriad Pro by Robert Slimbach and Carol Twombly, along with Fred Brady and Christopher Slye.

Body typeface: Arno Pro by Robert Slimbach.

Printer: Pollock Printing, Nashville, TN